MELTING POT
| OR |
CIVIL WAR?

MELTING POT
|OR|
CIVIL WAR?

**A SON OF IMMIGRANTS MAKES THE CASE
AGAINST OPEN BORDERS**

|||||||||||||

REIHAN SALAM

SENTINEL

Sentinel
An imprint of Penguin Random House LLC
375 Hudson Street
New York, New York 10014

Most Sentinel books are available at a discount when purchased in quantity for sales
promotions or corporate use. Special editions, which include personalized covers,
excerpts, and corporate imprints, can be created when purchased in large quantities.
For more information, please call (212) 572-2232 or e-mail specialmarkets@penguin
randomhouse.com. Your local bookstore can also assist with discounted bulk purchases
using the Penguin Random House corporate Business-to-Business program. For
assistance in locating a participating retailer, e-mail B2B@penguinrandomhouse.com.

Library of Congress Cataloging-in-Publication Data

Names: Salam, Reihan, author.
Title: Melting pot or civil war? : a son of immigrants makes the case against
    open borders / Reihan Salam.
Description: New York, New York : Sentinel, [2018]
Identifiers: LCCN 2018033512 | ISBN 9780735216273 (hardback)
Subjects: LCSH: United States—Emigration and immigration—Government policy. |
    BISAC: POLITICAL SCIENCE / Political Ideologies / Conservatism &
    Liberalism. | SOCIAL SCIENCE / Emigration & Immigration. | LAW /
    Emigration & Immigration.
Classification: LCC JV6483 .S25 2018 | DDC 325.73—dc23 LC record available at
https://lccn.loc.gov/2018033512

Printed in the United States of America
10 9 8 7 6 5 4 3 2 1

BOOK DESIGN BY LUCIA BERNARD

To my sisters

CONTENTS

MELTING POT
| OR |
CIVIL WAR?

Introduction

A few years ago, a cable news producer asked me to appear on his television program to discuss a grisly murder in which, if I recall correctly, a Muslim immigrant had hacked someone to death in the name of Islam. I begged off, partly because I had no special expertise in the matter. But as a professional pundit, that doesn't usually stop me: not only would I have happily discussed a swing Senate race or corporate tax cuts, but, if invited, I would also have gladly weighed in on the upcoming NATO military exercises in Romania or the latest developments in the Canadian–U.S. softwood lumber dispute. Nevertheless there was something about being asked to pontificate on this particular subject that gave me pause. Did my Muslim origins some-how make me an authority on terrorist violence? My opin-ions on Islamic extremism were, frankly, not all that unique. There were plenty of other journalists who knew far more about homegrown terrorism than I did, so I passed a few names along and politely declined to take part myself.

Then, in December 2017, another terror attack took place, only this time the culprit was someone who looked a lot like me. Akayed Ullah, a twenty-seven-year-old man born in Bangladesh, detonated a crudely designed explosive device in New York's Port Authority Bus Terminal, which sees more than 230,000 commuters every day. Thankfully, Ullah injured no one but himself. His intention, however, had evidently been to take as many of those commuters with him to the afterlife as he could. No one asked me to share my thoughts on the incident, which came as something of a relief. For a while, though, I could think of little else.

In the days and weeks that followed, dogged reporters, in the United States and in Ullah's native Bangladesh, pieced together a troubling story: though not notably radical before settling in Brooklyn in 2011, the young man had come to loathe America, and to see his true home as with the Islamic State, a gang of zealots best known for its homicidal brutal-ity. There was a sad irony in Ullah's devotion to IS. The Islamic State's propaganda insisted that it had built an egali-tarian paradise, where all Muslims were treated equally. In practice, while the terror group prized its European recruits and treated Arab volunteers relatively well, their African and South Asian counterparts, Bangladeshis very much included, were routinely treated as subhuman wretches. They were given the most dangerous assignments, the worst equipment, the lowest wages, and the lowest priority when it came to doling out jihadi war brides.[1] Yet Ullah apparently concluded that innocent U.S. commuters, including any number of recent immigrants much like himself, deserved to be put to death to avenge America's war against the Islamic State.

Why did I find Ullah's crime so affecting? For one, he lived in Kensington, the neighborhood where I grew up, and he was born in the same country as my parents. Ullah and I had shared the same stretches of sidewalk, and probably frequented the same corner stores. He settled in the country legally via a green card sponsored by a family member, not an uncommon story among Bangladeshi immigrants. When I saw Ullah's face, I saw someone who could have been a cousin, or who might have helped my mother carry an armful of groceries.

After I heard the news, I girded myself for what would come next. In the Age of Trump, all conversations about immigration descend into dueling spasms of culture-war outrage. As a poor Muslim immigrant turned lone-wolf terrorist, he was emblematic of some of the most polarizing aspects of the president's immigration agenda. Trump had famously campaigned on banning Muslim immigrants from the United States outright, a stance that enjoyed overwhelming support among GOP primary voters. As president, he called for curb-ing family-based admissions on the grounds that it meant admitting millions of immigrants lacking in "merit." Immi-gration advocates pushed back. Some argued that it was ob-scene to suggest that a man like Ullah was representative of immigrants at large. Others said that it was racist to question our current approach to family-based admissions.

And where was I? In an uncomfortable place. Donald Trump had built his political career on demonizing immi-grants, and I sympathized with immigration advocates who resented him for it. I am not just the son of immigrants. I am the brother, neighbor, and friend of immigrants, many of whom found Trump's rhetoric frightening. To the extent I harbor stereotypes about immigrants, they are positive. Some immigrants are violent and cruel, and others are feckless and lazy, just as there are many millions of natives who suffer from similar failings. But few are, like Akayed Ullah, intent on mass slaughter. Consider that he was mar-ried to a woman still living in Bangladesh, and his wife had recently given birth to a son.[2] She was applying for visas to join him in America. What could possibly have led him to bring such shame to his family members, and to destroy their prospects of a better life? Surely something so per-sonal and strange as to defy generalization or some specific public policy response.

So you'd think my sympathies would be with America's growing army of open borders activists, who call for ending all deportations and adopting ever more permissive immigration policies. Many of them are Americans like me, with recent immigration in their families, and I understand where they are coming from. But I noticed a contradiction in the arguments I was hearing for more open borders, which led me to part ways with the pro-immigration activists. There is a yawning chasm separating standard-issue immigration enthusiasts, who insist with a straight face that more open immigration policies will have absolutely no negative consequences, and an emerging class of intellectuals I call the bullet-biters: serious, rigorous, thoughtful immigration advocates who recognize that if the United States is going to welcome a far larger number of low-skill immigrants, we Americans will have to transform our welfare state, and we might even have to countenance the creation of a new class of guest workers who would be permanently barred from citizenship. The bullet-biters recognize that the world of the 2020s and 2030s will be drastically different from the world of the 1890s and 1900s, not least because the number of potential migrants to America will have greatly increased, and they forthrightly acknowledge that open borders and domestic equality simply can't coexist. Their position, in essence, is that by welcoming millions of low-skill workers who'd never be in a position to enter the U.S. middle class, we would greatly reduce *global* inequality while enriching native-born citizens, who'd be in a position to employ vast numbers of low-wage helpers, who could do menial jobs more cheaply and reliably than machines, at least until the machines get just a bit more sophisticated. Yes, this would mean the creation of an even more hierarchical society at home. But as far as the bullet-biters are concerned, that would be a small price to pay. I will have more to say about the arguments made by the bullet-biters in the chapters that follow. For now, though, I'll simply note that I found their case bracing and enlightening. It turns out that the standard-issue immigration activists—the ones who want more open immigration policies *and* a more equal society or, in other words, who want to have their cake and eat it, too—are crushingly naïve. They haven't really thought through where their convictions are taking them.

Which leads me back to Akayed Ullah. Though he was entirely unlike most immigrants in his hatefulness, there were other aspects of his story, or at least of what I could suss out, that were more familiar, and that reflect exactly the problems that have made me question the wisdom of our immigration system. Though Ullah had lived in the United States since 2011, he never quite established himself. He reportedly drove livery cabs and did occasional work as an electrician. Having known many immigrants who have made a living in backbreaking service jobs, I can attest that not everyone is cut out for dealing with customers and bosses. For prideful men who are accustomed to ruling the roost, service work is an endless series of humiliations. Despite living in one of the world's most diverse cities, Ullah's social world appears to have been limited to its Bengali-speaking enclaves. Described as "always angry" by a neighbor, Ullah didn't make much of an effort to befriend anyone outside of his enclave.[3] Understandably, he was in near-constant contact by phone with his wife back home. Ullah's hatefulness and lurch toward violence were unusual. His struggles as an immigrant in a country that placed little value on his skills and abilities, and that felt very far from home, were not.

These are familiar struggles for immigrants, most of them as nonviolent as you or me. The worst-off of these struggling millions live in illegal basement apartments, where they sleep in shifts, or in studios and one-bedroom apartments divvied up to accommodate five or six people, in conditions that resemble the tenements of yesteryear, or the teeming cities of the developing world. The very things that can make such a life easier to endure—being surrounded by coethnics who speak your native language, clinging tightly to loved ones back home—are often what keeps you on the margins. As far as the bullet-biters are concerned, this is perfectly fine. Immigrant poverty might be aesthetically displeasing, but these people are better off in absolute terms than they would be at home, and that is all that matters. That they are stuck on the bottom rungs of American society is—in a grand, global utilitarian calculus—immaterial.

To the rest of us, though, this is simply not tenable. We don't want an underclass that is forever locked out of middle-class prosperity. We are glad that immigrants are better off than they were in their native countries, yes, but we also worry about the children they raise on American soil, and what will happen to our society if impoverished immigrants give rise to an impoverished second generation that has no memory of life in the old country and who won't tolerate being relegated to second-class status.

And that is why I have come to believe that the United States badly needs a more thoughtful and balanced approach to immigration, including a greater emphasis on skills and a lesser one on extended family ties. I haven't come to this position lightly. Though my reasons might be different from Trump's, there is no getting around the fact that on the big picture question of whether we ought to make our immigration system more selective, I am closer to his position than to those of most of my friends and family members.

Immigration advocates tell us we have two choices: to be an open society that welcomes immigrants or a closed one that barricades itself off from rest of the world. If you disagree with any aspect of the pro-immigration agenda for any reason, you must be heartless or racist. Rhetorically and politically, forcing this choice is shrewd, but it is a false choice all the same. The real choice, I will argue, is whether we see the immigrants we welcome to our shores as permanent strangers to whom we have no real obligations other than to deliver them from the relative poverty of their homelands, or as free and equal citizens to whom we are pledging our loyalty in this generation and in those to come.

Strangers and Citizens

"Scripture tells us that we shall not oppress a stranger," said President Barack Obama, "for we know the heart of a stranger—we were strangers once, too.... And whether our forebears were strangers who crossed the Atlantic, or the Pacific, or the Rio Grande, we are here only because this country welcomed them in, and taught them that to be an American is about something more than what we look like, or what our last names are, or how we worship. What makes us Americans is our shared commitment to an ideal—that all of us are created equal, and all of us have the chance to make of our lives what we will."[4]

One of Obama's great talents was his unsurpassed ability to stack the rhetorical deck. Here he was announcing his executive order for deportation relief in 2014. To disagree with him was not just to reject his take on the costs and benefits of a particular policy, it was to oppress a stranger, which no less an authority than Scripture tells us is a very bad thing to do. Yet there was a small wrinkle in the former president's remarks. While calling on his fellow citizens to welcome the millions of strangers who make their way to our country to better their lives, he also insisted that his executive action would shield only those who'd been in the country unlawfully for five years or more. Moreover, it did not extend to those who might settle in the United States unlawfully in the future.

But surely those who've been in the country for, say, four years are strangers who deserve our compassion, too. Having praised unauthorized immigrants who work hard in low-paying jobs and who worship in our churches, the president must understand that there are tens of millions of people around the world who would gladly do the same, even if it meant risking their lives. According to one survey, there are roughly 700 million people around the world who would like to move permanently to another country, and 165 million of them say that their first choice would be to move to the United States.[5] My guess is that the vast majority of these aspiring immigrants are decent people who mean us no harm. If the Biblical injunction against oppressing a stranger is to serve as the lodestar of our immigration policy, why on earth would we set any limits at all?[6]

Obama's expansive language gave succor to open borders romantics—and to the most demagogic voices on the other side of the debate, up to and including the man who succeeded him in the White House. Together, these forces are making it all but impossible to craft a durable immigration compromise. The irony is that Obama had a different and more potent argument at his disposal, namely, that the young people to whom he was offering deportation relief weren't strangers at all. Because of our decades-long failure to enforce our immigration laws, an arrangement that suited unscrupulous low-wage employers just fine, they had become part of our communities. There was a perfectly good case for doing right by them while also embracing resolute enforcement, a case Obama gestured toward early in his presidency, yet which open borders activists came to angrily reject in its waning days. The result is that immigration policies championed by liberals and centrists as recently as the 2000s are now routinely denounced as unacceptably extreme.

Immigration policy is not about whether to be welcoming or hard-hearted. Short of absolutely open borders, which most advocates of *more* open borders at least claim to reject, it is about compromise. Like it or not, we need to weigh competing interests and moral goods, and to adjust our approach over time. An immigration policy that might have made sense in years past, when the labor market prospects of low-skill workers were much brighter, and when the number of working-class immigrants struggling to get by was much smaller, has entirely different implications today.

In the chapters that follow, I will offer a series of choices that go beyond open or closed. I'll begin by explaining the danger America faces if we don't find a way to return to the melting pot. I will then argue that we need to see immigration through a multigenerational lens. Policies that might make sense if we were indifferent to the fate of the children of immigrants won't make sense when we recognize that our future hinges on those later generations' well-being.

In chapter three, I describe the process of assimilation. Right now, immigrants and the children of immigrants represent roughly 25 percent of the U.S. population, a number set to rise considerably. And if anything, this number understates the cultural and political transformation to come, as many newcomers are quite young. How will these young Americans understand their place in the world? I contrast two different paths: *amalgamation*, in which second-generation Americans are fully incorporated into society's mainstream through ties of friendship and kinship, and *racialization*, in which they are relegated to second-class status. Racialization, I will argue, isn't just bad for the newcomers who bear the brunt of their own marginalization. It risks sparking a fearsome backlash from established Americans.

Next, I consider the long-term economic consequences of immigration. Its chief impact is not on the wages of native-born workers or on the raw size of the economy, though those issues tend to transfix people on both sides of the debate. Rather, at high enough levels, low-skill immigration affects the average skill level of the workforce, which in turn can encourage the de-engineering of the economy. Limits on low-skill immigration, in contrast, tend to spur offshoring and automation. Given widespread robophobia and anti-trade sentiment, many Americans would much prefer business models that rely on low-wage, low-skill labor over those built on high-wage, high-skill labor augmented by foreigners and increasingly intelligent machines. This, I will argue, is a serious mistake. I also suggest ways Americans can continue to invest in making the world outside America better even while limiting immigration.

The prescriptions I lay out are, frankly, pretty demanding, not just of government, but of all of us as citizens. We should admit immigrants only if we are fully committed to their integration and assimilation. Our number one priority should be ensuring that new arrivals and their loved ones can flourish as part of the American mainstream, not turning a blind eye as millions languish in poverty-stricken ghettos. That means fostering economic opportunity and a more inclusive American cultural identity. It means resisting class stratification and ethnic balkanization. The overall rate of immigration, the cultural and social capital immigrants bring with them, and the skills-composition of the immigrant influx as a whole all contribute to our chances of achieving this ambitious goal.

Ultimately, I want a country that does right by all of its citizens. America has been through challenging periods before, when it seemed as though the discontent of masses of urban immigrants might overturn the established order, and when older natives and younger newcomers were locked in cultural combat. Yet in earlier generations, at least some of our leaders had the wisdom to make the sacrifices necessary to knit a divided country back together. Just as the New Dealers found a way to unite the children of immigrants in smokestack cities with the descendants of settlers and the enslaved, we need to connect the fortunes of immigrant-rich communities, like the ones where I was raised, and the heartland, where coastal diversity is often looked on with suspicion.

As the historian Azar Gat has observed, most people are loyal first to immediate kin and then to larger kinship groups, like a clan or a tribe. The nations that have endured have done so by functioning as vastly extended kinship groups, whether literally, in the case of nations bound together by a shared belief in common descent, or figuratively, in the case of nations bound together by a shared belief in a common destiny. Over time, nations united by a common destiny tend to evolve into nations united by common descent. Inherited ethnic and cultural distinctions fade, and new hybrid ethnicities and cultures emerge. Not too long ago, we Americans referred to this process as "the melting pot." And we need it back, badly.

CHAPTER ONE

The Unfinished Melting Pot

In his 1908 play *The Melting Pot*, the playwright Israel Zangwill painted a romantic portrait of an America where *Mayflower* descendants and newcomers would come together as part of a compound nationality:[1] "Yes, East and West, and North and South, the palm and the pine, the pole and the equator, the crescent and the cross—how the great Alchemist melts and fuses them with his purging flame!" Yet the melting-pot ideal has long since fallen out of style, and it is easy to see why. For one, it was always conspicuously incomplete.[2]

Looking back, the United States wasn't much of a melting pot in the early 1900s, even if we limit ourselves to people of European descent. Though the country did attract large numbers of migrants in that era, mostly from Europe, many were sojourners, who came to the United States for a number of years to make their fortunes before returning to their homelands. Then there were the many migrants who lived among their co-ethnics in flourishing ethnic enclaves, which were regularly replenished by new arrivals. At their most vibrant, these enclaves were social worlds unto themselves, where migrants could speak their native languages and worship in familiar ways. Marrying outside one's own ethnic community was often frowned upon.

Only years later did the melting really begin in earnest. Following the immigration restriction legislation of the 1920s, European immigration slowed drastically, and ethnic enclaves around the country stopped being replenished. The children and grandchildren of European immigrants became much more likely to marry outside their ethnic tribes. While the offspring of these mixed marriages might have held on to some symbols of their cultural inheritances, they tended to identify more as American than anything else. By the 1950s, Americans from many different European ethnic groups were becoming part of a new compound ethnicity: they became, in short, white people. And for most whites, at least, midcentury America was defined by high and rising incomes and the widespread availability of dignified work. This era gave rise to the New Deal, and laid the economic and cultural foundation for the American Century.

The melting pot of old was whites-only, and most white Americans embraced racial segregation and the broader subjection of African Americans and other disadvantaged minorities to an inferior status. Indeed, part of what built solidaristic ties between native whites and European immigrants was common racism against blacks. In the decades since, most Americans have come to reject this whites-only conception of what it means to be an American without finding a broadly shared vision that can take its place. Some Americans, particularly older whites, look to midcentury America as their ideal, and see rising ethnic diversity as a threat to the country's predominantly white character. Others, mostly on the left, reject the idea that America should be understood as a single cultural nation, choosing instead to see it as a multicultural republic, in which separate and distinct groups vie for equal dignity and respect. What is missing is a unifying understanding of American nationhood.

To that end, the country needs a more expansive "melting pot" ideal, one that includes the descendants of slaves and of newcomers from around the world. As the author Michael Lind, who has championed this ideal for decades, has argued, the melting pot stands for "the voluntary blending of previously distinct groups into a new community"—a "great American mix" that draws on dozens of ethnicities and religious traditions. It is an ideal that rejects the arbitrary racial categories that have become so central to our cultural and political discourse.[3] By emphasizing all that Americans have in common, and the fact that integration and assimilation can, over time, deepen our shared cultural bonds, the melting pot ideal can pull us back from the brink of ethnic and class conflict.

The alternative to a new American melting pot is, I fear, an even more dangerously divided society. Lately, thinkers of various political stripes have taken to declaring that America is already in the midst of a kind of civil war. The conservative social critic Angelo Codevilla, writing in the *Claremont Review of Books*, warns that America's left-wing ruling class is waging a "cold civil war against a majority of the American people and their way of life."[4] On the other end of the political spectrum, journalist Peter Leyden and the political demographer Ruy Teixeira argue that our latter-day civil war pits retrograde white conservatives who fear the future against a multicultural alliance of pro-innovation progressives.[5] While Codevilla calls for lowering the temperature of America's cultural struggle, Leyden and Teixeira see victory in sight. For them, the only way forward is for the country's progressive majority to rise up and vanquish its aging white reactionaries once and for all. The shock of Trump's election has led many Americans, on the right and the left, to long for the metaphorical destruction of their domestic enemies. We see this in recurring fantasies of secession, and in an endless parade of fictional portrayals of nightmarish American futures, from *The Purge* to *The Handmaid's Tale.* Though it is still rare to hear respectable people say they want their political rivals dead, partisan enmity is such that it is not hard to imagine we will soon get there.

And, as Lind suggests, the false belief that America's racial and cultural boundaries are fixed is making matters worse. If non-Hispanic whites are an impermeable, unchanging group, it stands to reason that those who belong to that group would be alarmed by the fact that they will soon lose their majority status to a collection of hostile ethnic others. In an ethnically divided society, to be outnumbered is to be afraid. But if the boundaries between groups are fluid, and if distinctions between whites and nonwhites can be expected to fade away over time, as they would in a melting pot society, such concerns would be greatly reduced. Which will it be?

The Coming Crossover

Consider that among Americans under the age of eighteen, non-Hispanic whites will be in the minority by 2020.[6] Shortly thereafter, in 2032, a majority of working-age adults without college degrees, a decent proxy for the country's non-elite workforce, will be people of color.[7] As older, whiter generations fade away, they will be replaced by younger, less-white generations. This generational replacement will take place regardless of what happens to future immigration levels. As I write, the median age of non-Hispanic whites is forty-three, while that of Hispanics is twenty-eight. The median ages for blacks and Asians are thirty-three and thirty-six, respectively.[8] What this means is that a higher proportion of Hispanics, and to a lesser extent of blacks and Asians, are of childbearing age as compared to non-Hispanic whites.

Will the coming majority–minority crossover be positive and peaceful? The answer will depend on the pattern of assimilation during the coming decades. If newcomers are incorporated into the mainstream, the majority–minority crossover will be a non-event, as we'll wind up with a more expansive melting-pot majority, which will include Americans of all sorts of different ethnic backgrounds, non-European ethnic groups included. The bright lines separating disadvantaged groups from the mainstream will blur. But if newcomers instead find themselves marginalized, a much grimmer future lies ahead.

We see glimpses of this future in our most prosperous cities. Recently in Los Angeles, reporters Andrew Romano and Garance Franke-Ruta profiled anti-gentrification protesters, many of them second-generation Americans, who are adopting more radical methods to defend their neighborhoods, as they see it, from affluent outsiders.[9] Some of their tactics seem faintly comic, such as the expletive-laced

T-shirts condemning hipsters. But others involve threatening supposed interlopers and vandalizing property.

One could dismiss the new anti-gentrification radicalism as hooliganism. Romano and Franke-Ruta are more sympathetic, pointing to anger and disaffection among "poorer, nonwhite millennials who tend to live in major cities," and the soaring poverty rate among young adults with no more than a high school education, which, they note, increased threefold from 1979 to 2014. They observe that "roughly 70 percent of black families and 71 percent of Latino families don't have enough money saved to cover three months of living expenses." The same is true for only 34 percent of white families.[10] This contrast between wealth and poverty is particularly pronounced in gentrifying neighborhoods. "Ultimately," Romano and Franke-Ruta warn, "the fight over gentrification is what the fight over income inequality in America looks like up close today: a clash between the economic forces transforming our cities and a young, diverse, debt-saddled generation that is losing faith in capitalism itself."[11]

The activism we're seeing in Los Angeles, San Francisco, and other hotbeds of gentrification will spread. The visible manifestations of racial inequality are inciting many young Americans of color, and will incite them further as America goes through what some are calling "the Great Wealth Transfer."

Over the coming decades, baby boomers are set to pass

on $30 trillion in accumulated wealth to their heirs.[12] But this $30 trillion won't be divvied up evenly among younger Americans, for the obvious reason that rich boomer parents are disproportionately white, college-educated, native-born, and married. Families headed by someone who is middle-aged and was born to white parents, at least one of whom went to college, have a median income of $113,618. That is 2.7 times the income of nonwhite, non-college educated families. Meanwhile, the expected net worth of the most privileged is a full 14 times higher than that of the least privileged, at $374,640 compared to $26,718, according to the Federal Reserve Bank of St. Louis.[13]

In short, some people start out well ahead, even before their own education and accomplishments are taken into account. "Some of the inherited advantage," posits the St. Louis Fed, "plausibly flows through greater monetary transfers (in gifts and bequests) and more-intensive childhood investments, particularly in education, provided by college-educated parents who also are, in general, wealthier than nongrad parents." Beyond that, such families have greater savings, which can make them more resilient in times of trouble.

And then there are the millions of Americans living on the edge of poverty, many of whom are low-skill immigrants. Of course, most immigrants aren't fighting gentrification in the streets, for the obvious reason that they are typically more concerned with providing for their families.

Indeed, the great appeal of newcomers as workers is that relative to native-born workers, they will do any job and live in the most insalubrious conditions. This is especially true of low-skill immigrants, who greatly increase their incomes by moving to the United States, even when they are among the poorest of America's working poor. That's part of why the political influence of the newcomer working class is so muted as compared to that of the established working class. Low-income immigrants tend to naturalize at low levels, in part because many are so poor that the cost of naturalization is daunting,[14] and naturalized citizens vote at lower rates than the native-born.[15] Meanwhile, unauthorized immigrants have even less influence. If they were citizens raised with an expectation of fair and equal treatment, they would undoubtedly demand better wages and working conditions from their elite employers, and they'd have the political muscle to get their way at least some of the time. But, instead, they are forced to toil in the shadows. The relative powerlessness of foreign-born workers is a big part of what's made America's cosmopolitan cities so attractive to high-skill professionals.

But the citizen children of these workers won't be nearly as quiescent. Many of the poorer, nonwhite young people driving the new anti-gentrification radicalism are the children of low-skill immigrants who came to the United States with hope and stamina for sacrifice. It is possible to celebrate their sacrifices while recognizing that their children might reasonably have different attitudes toward their own economic travails. As someone born and raised in neighborhoods transformed by low-skill immigration, I can confirm that: "You're better off than you would have been had you been born in the Third World!" is not a satisfying riposte. "Gee, thanks. I also can't afford my rent."

Most of the poorest Americans are nonwhite, and that majority will continue to grow through the 2020s and 2030s.[16] Assuming present trends, meanwhile, America's rich will continue to be overwhelmingly white. Do you think working-class young Americans of color will shrug and accept their inherited disadvantage? Or will they be drawn to politicians who promise to do something about it, even if it means breaking with the established order?

It would be one thing if these young people were confident that mainstream Americans saw them as their equals. A lot of the time, though, they're not. In December 2017, Conor Williams, a liberal policy analyst and former schoolteacher, interviewed a group of high-achieving young students of color at a Brooklyn charter school. All were from immigrant families.[17] One of them, Esther Reyes, offered a heartfelt, stinging critique of the idea of the American Dream: "[T]he American dream we see in movies or in shows or in books, it's an American dream for white people . . . I think we could make a new version of the American dream if we wanted to, but just because of its history and the way that people have used it in the past, I don't think it exists."

Her doubts about America's promise are widespread among children raised in working-class immigrant households, and they didn't begin with the Trump presidency. Barring real reform, these young people will find themselves in a punishing economic environment, and they will have every reason to resent a power structure dominated by people who don't look like them and who aren't invested in their fate.

Immigrants are not to blame for the challenges we Americans face, which we have inherited from our forebears, and which we have made worse with our shortsightedness and greed. However, our current immigration system is increasing both the number and the share of children being raised in low-income households. If the children of immigrants were immune to the ill effects of growing up poor, this wouldn't be cause for concern. But the evidence suggests otherwise. Today's poor immigrants are raising tomorrow's poor natives, and we aren't doing nearly enough to break the cycle.

Just as Donald Trump's election spoke to the rage and disaffection of older whites in the heartland, the years to come may see a new populist revolt, driven by the resentments of working-class Americans of color. Imagine an America in which wealthy whites and Asians wall themselves off from the rest of society, and low-wage immigrants and their offspring constitute a new underclass. Working-class Americans of color will look upon their more privileged fellow citizens with envy, if not resentment, and better-off whites will look upon their poorer brown and black counterparts with fear and suspicion. Whites will embrace a more hard-edged white identity politics, and they will see efforts to redistribute their wealth as acts of racial aggression. Class politics will be color politics, and extremists on the left and the right will find millions of poor, angry youth willing to heed their calls to battle.

Toward a Middle-Class Melting Pot

There is another way. The key is understanding that diversity is not the problem. What is uniquely pernicious is *extreme between-group inequality*. There are many societies, such as Switzerland and Canada, that are home to a number of distinct ethnic groups, yet where interethnic relations are benign. Crucially, these are societies in which there aren't pronounced gaps in income and wealth between advantaged and disadvantaged groups, or where disadvantaged groups are relatively small in size. Under conditions of extreme between-group inequality, a different dynamic arises, in which disadvantaged groups can justly claim unfair treatment, and advantaged groups are keen to protect their status. Between-group inequality can be particularly dangerous when advantaged groups represent a shrinking share of the population relative to disadvantaged groups. That is America's present, and it is why we are entering such a dangerous moment.

So how do we pull back from the brink? By remaking the United States as a middle-class melting pot, in which the descendants of today's immigrants are fully incorporated into a multiracial mainstream. Though Americans will be of many different hues, as they are now, race will no longer determine their fate. Most Americans will have friends and family members from a wide array of backgrounds, and the ethnic distinctions that dominate our political and cultural life will fade. Rather than neglect the multigenerational poor on the implicit grounds that they are dispensable, we will break the cycle of poverty by building more integrated communities, in which all young people have a realistic prospect of leading happy and productive lives.

Whereas today's U.S. economy is divided between a privileged group of college-educated professionals and an insecure working class with little or no bargaining power and in constant fear of offshoring and automation, a middle-class melting pot would invest in the human capital of all Americans, especially the multigenerational poor. We would raise our average skill level, and instead of fearing the global economy and laborsaving technologies, we would embrace them.

To get there, though, we'd have to recognize an uncomfortable truth. High levels of low-skill immigration will make a middle-class melting pot impossible. For years, low-skill immigration has boosted the number of low-skill workers, and by extension the number of low-income households. Low-skill immigrants can increase their incomes dramatically by moving to the United States, but even then, they are likely to be poor by U.S. standards, for the simple reason that demand for low-skill labor in the United States is in secular decline. While low-skill immigration has greatly enriched immigrant workers themselves and the affluent professionals who rely on them most, this compositional effect has pushed up the poverty rate and kept large swaths of our economy stuck in a low-wage, low-productivity rut.

By limiting low-skill immigration, at least for a time, while welcoming high-skill immigration, we can change the dynamic. At the margin, doing so would ease wage pressures on established low-skill workers and make high-skill labor more abundant. Affluent professionals would face more competition, and they would surely resent it. Low-skill workers might face challenges, too, as rising wages would send employers scrambling to boost productivity. In time, though, a more selective, skills-based immigration system would yield a more egalitarian economy, in which machines do the dirty work and workers enjoy middle-class stability. And a more egalitarian economy would help heal our country's ethnic divides.

The divisions that define this moment in American history are not yet as worrisome as those that led to the

Civil War or the bloody battles pitting workers against industrialists at the dawn of the last century. Today, we do better by our poorest citizens and are combating discrimination. And if nothing else, we are rich enough to bribe our way out of conflict, at least for now.

Nevertheless, it is hard to shake the feeling that our luck might soon run out. To turn things around, we need to craft an immigration system that serves our long-term interests; we need to think not just about the people we bring to this country, but about their children, too.

CHAPTER TWO

Somebody Else's Babies

Shortly before I was born, my family visited Washington, DC, in the middle of a snowstorm. My poor mother, dodging snowbanks while pregnant, also had two little girls in tow. At one point, my mother tells me, she was confronted by an angry woman, who scolded her for having such a large family: "Don't you know there's a population crisis?" she asked. My mother replied that she fully intended to have a large family so that she and her offspring would displace America's native inhabitants, just as European settlers seized the lands of the American Indians. I'm not entirely sure the conversation went exactly as my mother describes it. But it does sound like the kind of thing she'd say in a fit of pique. That is one of the many reasons she is my hero.

My mother might find the prospect of an America overrun by little Salams delightful, and I rather like the idea myself, but not everyone welcomes the prospect. I thought of her when, in 2017, Steve King, an Iowa congressman known for his strident opposition to immigration, tweeted, "We can't restore our civilization with somebody else's babies." King's remark was widely denounced.[1] It came not long after Donald Trump's inauguration, at a moment when the immigration debate felt even more combustible than usual, and it raised disturbing questions. What did King mean by "somebody else's babies"? Was the congressman implying that the children of immigrants, or the children of Muslims or nonwhites, are not our babies? I can hardly blame King's critics for drawing that conclusion. My takeaway was that if not for babies, the immigration debate wouldn't be nearly as contentious.

Imagine if the United States admitted only immigrants who, for whatever reason, had no interest in having children. Though many of these immigrants would do great things, their collective impact on American society would be muted, for the simple reason that it would last only one generation. Immigrants would come to the United States as fully formed adults, work for a few years, and then vanish. But that's not how it works. Immigrants do have children, and they tend to have more of them than the native-born.[2] Native-born Americans are forming families later in life, if at all, and they're having fewer children as a result. America is thus in the middle of a birth dearth.[3]

One consequence is that recent immigrants, with their comparatively healthy birthrates, are having an outsized impact on America's younger generations. One in four U.S. children under the age of eighteen has at least one foreign-born parent. Unless native-born Americans start having many more babies, a prospect that for now seems rather remote, new immigrants and their descendants will account for almost 90 percent of all population growth between now and 2065.[4] That's a dramatic turn from just a few decades ago, when immigration was an abstraction for most Americans, who lived in neighborhoods and towns largely untouched by it.

Steve King—born in rural Iowa in 1949, at a time when immigration levels were extremely low, and raised and educated when the foreign-born share of the U.S. population was still falling from the heights reached in the early 1900s—no doubt laments this development. Many others, however, love it. If established Americans aren't having babies, then perhaps we should be grateful that newcomers are doing the hard work of raising the next generation.

But what exactly does it mean for babies to be *ours*? If a baby—brown or white, Christian or Hindu—is ours, do we congratulate ourselves on having one more baby, and move on? Or does "owning" that baby mean we have concrete, tangible obligations to it, and to its parents and the communities it will join? Are we willing to pay higher taxes to help ensure our babies are well fed, or do we expect the parents of our babies to fend for themselves, even in the leanest of times? This, to my mind, is one of the most important questions in the immigration debate, yet it's a question we tend to dodge.

Starting from the Bottom

America's child poverty levels are obscene. We are not doing right by our babies, and we haven't done right by them for a long while. In 2012, the percentage of those under eighteen living in poverty in the United States was 20.5, closer to Mexico (25.8 percent) and Turkey (28.4 percent) than the United Kingdom (9.5 percent), Germany (8.1 percent), or Denmark (3.8 percent).[5] But as the scholar Kay Hymowitz has observed, the United States is different from those other countries in a way that might be relevant to our failures: "Before Europe's recent migration crisis, the United States was the only developed country consistently to import millions of very poor, low-skilled families, from some of the most destitute places on earth—especially from undeveloped areas of Latin America—into its communities, schools, and hospitals."[6]

Modern America's relative openness to low-skill newcomers can be traced back to the 1965 Immigration and Naturalization Act, which codified family preference and after which immigrant children were more likely to be poor than native children. (The opposite had been true during the age of immigration restriction.) Of course, the United States was already an outlier in child poverty—poverty among black children reached almost 47 percent in the 1990s. However, history does suggest, as Hymowitz writes, that "you can allow mass low-skilled immigration, which many on the left and the right—and probably most poverty mavens—consider humane and quintessentially American. But if you do, pursuing the equally humane goal of substantially reducing child poverty becomes a lot harder."[7]

This is certainly not to suggest that *all* of the children of immigrants are poor, or even most. Nevertheless, the numbers tell a sobering story. The United States is home to eighteen million people under the age of eighteen who are either the children of immigrants or are immigrants themselves. According to research by the Annie E. Casey Foundation, the median income for these families is 20 percent lower than for established families. In fact, "only 47 percent of children in immigrant families live in households with incomes above 200 percent of poverty. This means that more than half struggle to make ends meet."[8] It is tragic but not surprising, then, that although children of immigrants make up 24 percent of the United States' youth population, they represent 30 percent of all low-income children, and only 62 percent of them live in low-poverty areas. (The national figure is 70 percent.)[9]

It will be difficult for them to escape poverty. For one, "eight out of 10 are children and youths of color," the report states, and they "face many of the systemic and institutional barriers faced by other children of color living in the United States."[10] These children also face formidable obstacles when attending school. It is generally accepted that it is more expensive to provide the same quality of education to disadvantaged kids than to those from better-off families. For one, high-poverty schools often have a hard time attracting and retaining the best teachers, and poor children are more likely to need social services. Among immigrant families, only 70 percent of children live with someone who has a high school diploma or better. It is less likely that the children in immigrant families who don't will complete college. Meanwhile, only 8 percent of fourth graders in immigrant families are proficient in reading. Only 5 percent of eighth graders are proficient in math. That compares to a still dismally low 38 percent and 34 percent for children with U.S.–born parents.[11]

Today's poor immigrants are facing headwinds that immigrants in midcentury America did not, and the implications for their children are worrisome, to say the least.

Welcoming immigrants is pretty easy if all it means is

giving them a menial job and a social security number. All we have to do is let potential migrants know that they'll be allowed to live and work in peace. If you believe you will be even slightly better off in America, and if you are willing to make the personal sacrifices leaving your loved ones behind will entail—sacrifices that are much smaller in the age of cheap flights and even cheaper calls—you have every reason to immigrate. Thanks to low minimum wages, a lightly regulated labor market, and a seemingly bottomless appetite for cheap services, we Americans can put just about any immigrant to work, especially if they are willing to do jobs even the poorest Americans are reluctant to take on.

The tricky part comes when immigrants form families in America, and their children, who never affirmatively chose to immigrate, start expecting more. It is one thing for immigrants to live in substandard housing, spend a lifetime toiling on the bottom rungs of the jobs ladder, and never earn enough to climb into the middle class. These are people who have made the calculation that they'd be better off leaving home, and that living as a poor person in America is a heck of a lot better than the alternative. We can hardly begrudge them that. But it is another for generation after generation of children born in the United States to be stuck in straitened circumstances. If welcoming immigrants is easy, we are about to discover that living up to the expectations of the children of immigrants will be hard. Everything changes in the next generation, when the babies—*our* babies—grow up.

The Model Minority Illusion

There is a widespread belief that immigrants and their off-spring have poverty-defying superpowers that natives do not. That is certainly the impression you'd get from pundits and lobbyists who celebrate all the Silicon Valley technology entrepreneurs who were born abroad, or the fact that immigrant scientists seem to have a presumptive lock on every year's Nobel Prizes.

But immigrants are humans, and like most successful humans, they do better if they start with huge advantages. Spectacular immigrant success stories—the billionaire entrepreneurs, the Nobel Prize winners—often *start* in rich and urbanized societies, such as Israel, Taiwan, Canada, and Europe's market democracies, where future immigrants acquire skills that are readily transferable to the United States. The superstar immigrants who do come from developing countries are typically raised in families drawn from the best-off, most well-educated strata of their homelands.

There is no question that a disproportionately large share of immigrants are impoverished[12] and that many arrive in the United States with minimal schooling and poor English-language skills.[13] Why, then, are we so fixated on a minority of high-achieving immigrants and their children? My theory is that while the child of well-off immigrants who wins the science fair tells us exactly what we want to hear about ourselves, the one who doesn't have enough to eat is a rebuke: a reminder that rags-to-riches stories delight and inspire us precisely because they are so rare. The fact that Sergey Brin, the celebrated cofounder of Google, was born in Russia (to parents who were accomplished scholars) is a feel-good story. The fact that 70 percent of Hispanic infants in America are born to mothers with a high school diploma or less, most of whom are either in or near poverty, is a feel-bad story.[14]

As Cynthia Feliciano, a sociologist at the University of California, Irvine, has long argued, the pre-migration lives of immigrants matter for the lives they lead in America.[15] Most immigrants to the United States come from countries with low levels of education, so even immigrants with no more than a high school education might have been more educated than non-migrants in their native country. In other words, these immigrants have been positively selected. Immigrants who are less educated than the typical non-migrant in their native country are, in contrast, negatively selected. According to Feliciano, immigrants who enjoyed higher status *before* they arrived in the United States often set high expectations for their U.S.–born children, which in turn can help insulate them from some of the headwinds associated with growing up poor in America.

Yet there is a big difference between immigrants who are

drawn from the best-off, most well-educated strata of their homelands, and those who hail from, say, the top half. Indian immigrants, for example, have benefited from what the scholars Sanjoy Chakravorty, Devesh Kapur, and Nirvikar Singh call a "triple" selection process.[16] Most now enter the United States via high-skill worker visas, which ensures that they have much higher incomes than low-skill immigrants; these high-skill workers have made it through India's intensely competitive higher education system, which serves only a small fraction of its population; and the Indians who have access to higher education in the first place tend to be those from better-off families. In 2003, Kapur found that whereas India's highest castes—including, most famously, its Brahmins—represent less than 3 percent of its population, they account for 45 percent of Indian immigrants in the United States. Meanwhile, members of India's most disadvantaged groups, to which one-third of Indians belong, account for a mere 1.5 percent of Indian immigrants. When observers marvel at the success of America's Indian immigrants, and point to it as a sign that anyone from anywhere can thrive in twenty-first-century America, they tend to neglect the fact that this so-called model minority is almost entirely an artifact of selection.

The role of selection is not limited to Indian immigrants. The Stanford economist Edward Lazear, a champion of high immigration levels, has found that it is not the supposed "quality" of a given country that determines how well its immigrants fare in the United States.[17] Rather, outcomes for different immigrant groups are in large part a matter of selection: "The larger the number of immigrants from an origin country, the lower the level of educational attainment, of wages and of earnings in the U.S. The larger the population of the origin country, the higher the educational attainment, the higher the wages and the higher the earnings of those immigrants in the U.S." In other words, the harder it is to enter the United States as an immigrant from a given country, the more likely it is that immigrants will be drawn from the top of their country of origin's social pecking order.

Conversely, the easier it is to the enter the United States from a given country, the more likely it is that immigrants from that country will come from poorer, less-educated families, who will likely find it difficult to vault into the middle class. It is not superior "Asian values" that account for the fact that, for example, second-generation Chinese Americans earn much higher incomes than second-generation Mexican Americans. A more parsimonious explanation is simply that Chinese immigrants are far more likely to have come from their country's educational elite than Mexican immigrants and have passed that advantage down to their children.[18]

It is tempting to believe that the challenges facing impoverished immigrants are easily overcome. After all, European immigrants in the 1900s were similarly downtrodden, yet their families managed to join the American middle class in two or three generations. The problem is that the structure of the U.S. economy has changed. In those days, fewer Americans had completed high school, so Europeans faced less of a skills deficit compared to the established population. These days, though, high school and even college have become the norm for Americans, which puts new arrivals with limited education at a greater disadvantage. Worse still, the difference in earnings between those with advanced degrees and low-skill workers has risen astronomically in the century between the great wave of European migration and now.[19] In fact, since the 1980s, real wages for men without high school diplomas have by some measures fallen.

It is thus much harder for poorer new arrivals and their offspring to climb out of poverty. The average male Mexican immigrant arrives in the United States with 9.4 years of schooling. That rises in the second generation, but to only 12.6 years. The numbers flatline or decline in the third generation.[20] There is no reason to expect that these immigrants will have an easier time than any other American without a college degree. And they don't: for immigrants and their descendants with twelve years of schooling or fewer, employment rates decrease from the first to the second generation and from the second generation to the third.[21] In turn, immigrants start out earning less than established Americans with similar skills, and although their incomes go up over time, they never quite catch up to those of their established brethren.[22] Nor does progress made in the first generation, especially for Mexican and Central American immigrants, necessarily continue into the second and third.[23]

According to data collected 2013, meanwhile, poverty rates among immigrants start high at almost 19 percent, and remain near 15 percent for second-generation Americans and 12 percent for those in the third generation.[24] Those figures are even more extreme for people of Mexican and Central American origin.[25] Perhaps relatedly, although the crime rate among immigrants is lower than among the established population, it ticks up in subsequent generations.[26] Immigrants settle in the United States with a sense of hope and purpose. Their children, particularly those raised in disadvantaged neighborhoods, grow up with a much bleaker perspective on the American Dream. Could this reflect the fact that while immigrants are grateful for the opportunity to live in America, their children and grandchildren have a less romantic sense of what it means to grow up on the bottom rungs of our society? I believe the answer is yes.

There are those who suggest that the intergenerational transmission of poverty is a concern only among immigrants from Mexico, Central America, and the Caribbean, as the second-generation members of many other contemporary immigrant groups fare about as well as the typical American.[27] But this is shortsighted. It neglects the fact that average outcomes for immigrant groups are shaped by selection. Under current U.S. immigration law, as we will discuss, most new green cards are issued to the relatives of U.S. immigrants and lawful permanent residents, who are chosen without regard for their skills. As an immigrant group gains a foothold, and as family-sponsored immigrants come to outnumber those who enter the United States through more selective channels, it is reasonable to expect average outcomes to drift downwards. Further, the notion that Hispanic immigrant families are the only ones facing serious obstacles to upward mobility insultingly implies that there is something defective about their culture. In fact, high-skill immigrants from Latin America are thriving, and low-skill immigrants from Asia and elsewhere face an uphill climb.

Elite immigrants and struggling immigrants aren't defying the logic of America's caste system. They and their children are being incorporated into it. The children of struggling immigrants tend to struggle. The children of elite immigrants make their way into America's elite, where they add a much-needed dash of superficial diversity—just enough to make us forget their inconvenient working-class counterparts. As much as we might want to believe that Americans of all backgrounds have it in their power to succeed, the data paint a less rosy picture. Children raised in poor families are dramatically more likely to grow up to be poor adults than children raised in better-off families.[28] If you're raised by poor parents in a poor neighborhood, the odds are against you.

Our Babies, Our Responsibility

One response to the challenges facing poor immigrant families is to counsel self-reliance: if immigrant parents don't have the wherewithal to succeed, that is their problem alone. By this standard, all babies other than one's very own are somebody else's babies.

But that kind of thinking will lead to ruin as the younger generation comes of age. For one, there is ample evidence that impoverished children have a much harder time gaining the skills they need to make a good living as adults.[29] Society as a whole will pay the price if they are unable to realize their full potential. Parents who shirk their duties may well deserve our scorn. The same can't be said of the millions of parents who want to do right by their children, but who simply cannot by dint of their limited resources. As skills and resources and networks are passed on from one generation to the next, the difference in well-being between adults who are the products of generations of stability and success and those who are products of generations of instability and disappointment will grow larger and larger.

On one side of the divide are families that are in an ideal position to cultivate non-cognitive skills—a sense of motivation and self-control, among other things—in their children. Those families can accumulate savings and maintain strong networks of friends and extended family members.

On the other side of the divide are families that are poor, isolated from the cultural mainstream, and subject to extreme stress. Those families will struggle to survive and to keep their children out of harm's way. This division is already undermining the legitimacy of our democracy.

That is ultimately why modern America assumes some level of collective responsibility for the well-being of all citizens, regardless of their country of origin or the legal status of their parents. And it is why there is growing support for anti-poverty spending among all Americans, and especially among newcomers.[30]

But that's not to suggest anti-poverty spending is some kind of panacea. The expansion of the welfare state has meant that responsibilities that had once been the purview of families and communities now belong to government. Social Security, for example, was designed to address poverty among the aged, as older Americans outlived their meager savings and adult children either could not or would not take on the responsibility of providing care. Medicaid aimed to provide medical care to the poor, a responsibility that had traditionally been met by a patchwork of local charities and governments.

Yet even as families have seen some of these burdens eased, their ability to meet other responsibilities, like instilling the value of discipline and deferred gratification in young children, appears to have eroded. The goal of universal early education, for example, has gained momentum because of the perception that many children are raised in chaotic environments and thus lack the non-cognitive skills that are necessary to persevere through high school and meet professional obligations. The hope is that immersing poor children in a structured learning environment will help build these skills, and isolate them from the chaos of home. Paid parental leave and wage subsidies, policies that have champions on the right and the left, are designed to get families through crises when they don't have networks of relatives and friends they can rely on.

Just as professional households outsource work that had once been done in the home by eating out or by hiring professional cleaners, a cynic might argue that the expansion of the welfare state is fundamentally about outsourcing the responsibility to plan ahead, to form strong, lasting relationships, and, increasingly, to raise children who are capable of becoming self-reliant adults. Small-government conservatives might regret the growing role of government in subsidizing low-income families, but that doesn't change the fact that the social safety net is here to stay. If anything, its role is set to expand. As the labor market prospects of low-skill workers have deteriorated, government has stepped in to help them meet their needs and, more important, the needs of their children. For example, a full-time minimum wage worker in the United States earns an annual salary of $14,500.[31] If this worker is the sole breadwinner for a two-parent, two-child family, and if she is authorized to work in the United States, she is entitled to a number of federal tax credits, including the earned-income tax credit and the child credit. After taking these credits into account, her family's after-tax income would be $24,600. I support these tax credits, and I believe they should be more generous. There is no getting around the fact that they make a big difference in the lives of low-wage workers. Without them, these workers would be dramatically worse off.

However, providing such support to the second- and third-generation descendants of impoverished immigrants has the potential to get very expensive as those groups expand. It was in part to avoid such costs that the "public charge" test was introduced.

Immigration Yes, Welfare No?

In theory, at least, all non-refugee immigrants to the United States are required to pass the "public charge" test.[32] According to a long-standing federal policy, potential immigrants will be barred from the United States if they are likely to become dependent on public assistance. If an immigrant does become a public charge within five years of arriving in the country for reasons that can't be attributed to, say, a disability she developed after settling in the United States, she can, in principle, be deported. The idea is that U.S. taxpayers can reasonably expect that immigrants who chose to settle in America can provide for themselves. The public charge test could be understood as the way American policymakers of the past tried to ensure that a multigenerational immigration system wouldn't prove burdensome.

Of course, the actual effects of this policy hinge on the definition of a public charge, and in practice it has been defined by the executive branch. In 1999, the Clinton administration put in place guidelines that defined a public charge very narrowly as someone who is "primarily dependent on the government for subsistence, as demonstrated by either: (i) the receipt of public cash assistance for income maintenance or (ii) institutionalization for long-term care at government expense."[33] Are you dependent on public assistance if, say, you receive Medicaid, SNAP, or public housing? Not according to the Clinton guidelines, which put those social services programs in a different category from cash assistance—a standard that remained intact under Presidents George W. Bush and Barack Obama. Few aspiring immigrants are turned away on the grounds that they might become a public charge, and almost no one has been deported on that basis in years.

Why did the Clinton guidelines define public charges so narrowly? And why have these lax rules persisted? The simplest explanation is that when you impose a stringent public charge definition, you are not just keeping immigrants out of the country. You are infuriating their U.S. citizen relatives.

One result of our permissive interpretation of the public charge test is that, as some of the more forthright advocates for low-skill immigration will acknowledge, a strikingly large share has non-citizens—somewhere between one in three and one in two—have incomes low enough to qualify either them or their dependents for means-tested programs, such as food stamps or CHIP.[34] To be sure, non-citizens are barred from the use of some of these programs during their first years in the country. And even when non-citizens are eligible for SNAP or cash assistance, immigrant-headed families are less likely to access them than equally poor families headed by natives. Immigrants are often less aware of the benefits that are available to them, due to social isolation or language barriers. What is odd is that immigration advocates will at times suggest that it's a *good* thing that impoverished non-citizens aren't aware that there are eligible safety-net benefits that could better the lives of their kids.[35]

There is another twist in the story, which is that in the 1996 welfare reform legislation, Congress included a number of provisions aimed at curbing immigrant use of public assistance. Though widely condemned as draconian, these provisions were in fact a successful attempt on the part of pro-immigration Republicans, led by libertarians and Christian conservatives, to head off efforts by the GOP's restrictionist wing to reduce immigration levels. The idea was to make high immigration levels more palatable to moderate and restrictionist voters by ensuring that immigrants wouldn't drain public resources.

The centerpiece of this "immigration yes, welfare no" agenda was a five-year ban on means-tested benefits for new legal immigrants. In addition, lawful permanent residents sponsored by a family member were required not just to report their own income, but to report the income of their sponsors as well. It was the combined income of immigrants and their sponsors that would determine the immigrants' eligibility for means-tested programs, a concept known as "sponsor deeming." To further deter immigrants from making use of public assistance, government agencies were authorized to seek repayment from sponsors for benefits paid to sponsored immigrants, a concept known as "sponsor recovery." Nevertheless, in the years that followed, limits on means-tested benefits were softened while sponsor recovery was hardly ever tried, not least out of fear of political blowback.

"Immigration yes, welfare no" was a wildly successful slogan, but it hasn't amounted to much in practice. Denying low-income immigrants SNAP benefits hasn't deterred low-skill immigrants from settling in the country, for the obvious reason that they still make a lot more in the United States than they would have at home, even without food stamps. The main effect of the five-year ban seems to have been that it has made the developmental health outcomes for the children raised in these households a bit worse than they would have been otherwise, despite the fact that eligibility for children of immigrant parents was left untouched.[36] Arloc Sherman and Danilo Trisi of the Center for Budget and Policy Priorities have observed that the five-year waiting period has contributed to a sharp rise in food insecurity and deep poverty rates for non-citizens and children living with non-citizen parents, even though only about one-sixth of legal immigrants have been in the country for five years or fewer.[37]

What if "immigration yes, welfare no" became more than just a slogan—what if it were really possible to strip *all* immigrant-headed households of SNAP benefits, leaving aside the myriad other benefits for which low-income households are eligible? In a comprehensive report on the economic and fiscal impact of immigration, the National Academy of Sciences found that 45.3 percent of immigrant-headed households with children relied on food assistance as compared to 30.6 percent of native-headed households with children.[38] Taking food assistance away from these families wouldn't just mildly inconvenience them. The economists Hilary Hoynes of the University of California, Berkeley, Diane Whitmore Schanzenbach of Northwestern University, and Douglas Almond of Columbia University found that access to food stamps has long-lasting effects on the well-being of children raised in low-income households, including significant reductions in obesity, high blood pressure, and diabetes—serious chronic illnesses that can reduce earning potential and generate substantial medical costs.[39]

Benefits and Burdens

Say you agree that we as a country ought to provide for low-income immigrants and their children. What would that mean for taxpayers? A 2017 report from the National Academies of Sciences, Engineering, and Medicine made an earnest attempt to answer that question.

At the top level, according to the study, the answer depends on the health of the economy at the time of the immigrants' arrival and on the state they land in, since each has its own policies and economic ecosystem. Age at arrival also matters; that will determine how long immigrants will be in the workforce and thus how many years they'll pay income taxes. It will also determine what support they will need from the government, and at which level. "Whereas state and local governments tend to support programs for the young, the federal government's fiscal responsibility falls disproportionately on programs for the elderly—specifically pensions and health care—which occur later in life," notes the NAS study. "When immigrants are on average younger than the population as a whole—as has traditionally been true (though this is changing somewhat in recent decades)—states tend to incur the more immediate costs of new immigrants."[40]

And then there are all of the questions about how you will assign debits and credits, and over what time period. You might want a snapshot of a single year, but if that year sees a disproportionate number of school-age immigrants, immigrants as a whole might look like more of a burden than they could turn out to be over many years. Running a long-term projection could address that issue, but it would include thousands of assumptions about the future of policy, the economy, immigrant fertility, educational attainment, death and return rates, and so on. There's also the tricky question of the unit of study: household or individual. The makeup of a household can change over time, which renders it inappropriate for longer-term projections, but many public goods are better thought of as being consumed by a family unit. Making things more complicated, in some cases, it makes sense to allocate the cost of public goods on an even per capita basis. For example, the cost of healthcare and school are basically proportional to the number of consumers. For other services, though, like national security, the marginal cost of adding one more immigrant is near zero. And finally, there are unpredictable variables such as the pressure immigrants could add on housing prices, congestion, and so on.

Because of all of the assumptions inherent in any accounting of the fiscal impact of immigration, the NAS study warns, the results will be more useful as a way to compare groups rather than to arrive at absolute estimates. One scenario, which looked at the 2013 outlays, included three groups: the first-generation immigrants and their dependents, the second generation and dependents, and the third-plus generation and dependents. All three groups were revealed to be net fiscal burdens, although the first generation had the lowest ratio of credits to debits. In fact, the first generation accounted for almost 18 percent of the population but closer to 22 percent of the deficit.[41] (The calculation assigned costs for public goods on an average per capita basis.)

In another scenario—this one longitudinal, not including pure public goods, and assuming taxes and growth in the size of government are in line with historical precedent—NAS found vastly different net present value flows for immigrant groups depending on educational attainment. The average immigrant with less than a high school degree can be expected to cost $115,000 dollars over a seventy-five-year period. That immigrant's descendants, if they also have less than a high school diploma, will cost $70,000 dollars. Meanwhile, the net contribution of an immigrant with a bachelor's degree is $210,000, with descendants making net contributions of $42,000, assuming they also have bachelor's degrees.[42] It is worth noting that established Americans show a similar spread. If anything, NAS finds, those without a high school diploma are costlier, simply because they are eligible for more government programs.

If we were to make the tax code more steeply progressive while increasing redistribution to low-income households, the net fiscal impact of low-skill immigration would only get worse, at least for the foreseeable future.[43] What do universal pre-K, subsidized child care, and Medicare for

All all have in common? They cost money, and the taxes paid by low-income immigrants wouldn't come close to paying for the benefits they'd be receiving. Some immigration advocates insist that the children of poor immigrants will automatically vault into the bourgeoisie, closing the fiscal gap and then some. Perhaps they are right. But as we've seen, the children of poor immigrants face challenges of their own. The NAS study projects that of the children of foreign-born parents with less than a high school education, only 6.2 percent will graduate from college.[44] Low incomes in one generation risk extending to the next.

Since the NAS report was released, voices on all sides of the immigration debate have tried to spin its findings to make their case. My interpretation is straightforward: whereas a more selective, skills-based immigration system would prove a fiscal boon, a system that selects immigrants with little regard for their lifelong earning potential, or the needs of their families, is more likely to prove a burden.

The Qatar Solution

Of course, there is another way to deal with the multigenerational impact of migration, and that is to ensure that migrants are never in a position to start families on U.S. soil. While most Americans take for granted that immigrants and the babies of immigrants are a package deal, this is not necessarily the case. There is a big difference between what I will call multigenerational immigration systems, in which it is assumed that immigrants and their descendants will become members of the body politic, and monogenerational systems, in which there is no such expectation, and indeed there can be active efforts to prevent migrants from putting down roots.

America's immigration system is multigenerational almost by default. According to most experts, the Fourteenth Amendment compels the U.S. government to grant citizenship to all children born on U.S. soil, regardless of the legal status of their parents. One result is that the United States is home to large numbers of mixed-status households, in which U.S. citizen children are being raised by loved ones who do not have legal status.[45] Needless to say, separating citizen children from their parents is a charged issue, and it's a central part of why so many Americans favor a sweeping amnesty for unauthorized immigrants. It is also why a number of other market democracies, such as Australia, Britain, France, Ireland, and New Zealand, have ended automatic birthright citizenship and tried to ensure that the only babies with citizenship are the babies of individuals lawfully present in their countries or of citizens who find themselves abroad.

It's possible to go further still in the direction of separating openness to immigrants from openness to their babies. A number of countries have designed their immigration systems to, in effect, shed any responsibility for the babies of migrants. Some, particularly in the Arabian Gulf, do this by recruiting guest workers rather than admitting immigrants on a permanent basis. Almost by definition, guest workers can be deported as soon as they become burdensome. It is common for guest workers to live in gender-segregated facilities, in part to reduce the likelihood that they will form family ties. In Qatar, for example, restrictive employment contracts severely limit the ability of migrant workers to even visit their families back home. While well-paid employees are allowed to sponsor dependents to join them in Qatar, there is almost no path for migrant workers or their offspring to become naturalized citizens.[46] Indeed, it was only recently that the children of Qatari women with non-Qatari fathers were granted permanent residency status.[47] In short, Steve King has nothing on the Qataris when it comes to distinguishing between their babies and somebody else's.

At the same time, though, Qatar is extremely open to migrant labor. Roughly 94 percent—yes, 94 percent—of Qatar's workforce, and 70 percent of its population, is foreign-born. Martin Ruhs, one of the world's foremost migration experts, has observed that as a general rule, countries are either inclusive when it comes to admitting immigrants and stingy when it comes to making the sacrifices it would take to ensure their full participation in society, or they take a more selective approach to admissions while treating immigrants more generously.[48] This is an idea to which we will return. For now, just keep in mind that if every migrant worker in the Arabian Gulf was not just a worker but the potential parent of a little baby citizen—who would be entitled to all the rights and privileges of any other citizen—you can bet Qatar's borders wouldn't be quite so open.

From an open borders perspective, the only relevant question in immigration policy is whether the people who now enjoy the fruits of participation in our prosperous society are any more morally praiseworthy than the vast number of potential immigrants we turn away. If they are not, there can be no justification for mass exclusion—the flipside of any controlled immigration regime. In this view, it's not at all obvious that America's multigenerational approach is superior to Qatar's monogenerational one. Even barring migrants and their offspring from citizenship is better than excluding them from the country outright, or so the argument goes.[49]

But there's a pretty straightforward reason the most open countries in the world, such as Qatar, bar migrants and their offspring from citizenship. If Qatar allowed its migrant workers to become equal members of the political community, they would undoubtedly use their political power to redress their inferior status. The descendants of migrants would be even less inclined to tolerate extreme inequality. The Qataris aren't foolish. They understand this, which is why they are so reluctant to let go of their monogenerational approach, even when it attracts opprobrium from the international press.[50]

Then there are countries, like Canada, Australia, and Singapore, that take a hybrid approach, operating multigenerational and monogenerational immigration systems in parallel. The multigenerational systems are for high-skill immigrants, who are selected largely on the basis of their lifelong earning potential. High-skill immigrants find it much easier to acquire permanent residency, and their children are either granted citizenship automatically or they are given an easy path to acquiring it. The monogenerational systems, meanwhile, are reserved for low-skill immigrants, who are either forbidden from bringing spouses and children with them or discouraged from doing so.[51]

What is it that motivates this two-tiered approach? It's presumably not racism, as all three countries welcome a diverse array of high-skill immigrants. One explanation is that like the Qataris, these countries implicitly recognize that taking on a collective obligation that is multigenerational means quite a bit more than taking on one that is monogenerational, and so they are intent on limiting the downside risks of extending full citizenship rights to newcomers by ensuring, to the best of their ability, that the newcomers will be capable of supporting themselves.

America, as we have established, mostly eschews a monogenerational approach. And there is a good reason for that.

As the political scientist Morris Levy suggested to *The New York Times*, Americans "dislike the idea of a permanent second-class citizen," as it cuts against "a core set of values that people think of as really elemental to being American."[52] The United States does have long-term guest-worker programs, to be sure, but they typically give guest workers the right to bring over their dependents. Overstaying guest-worker visas is common, and, of course, people on temporary visas often have citizen children. The babies of low-skill immigrants are as much our babies as the babies of high-skill immigrants. And, as of now, we are letting them down.

CHAPTER THREE

Race to the Bottom

As a little kid, I was an accidental ethnic pioneer. On the first day of kindergarten, I remember being teased for being an "Indian," which is to say an indigenous person. I vaguely recall that my family found the teasing more baffling than offensive, and so I brushed it off. In short order, the teasing stopped and I befriended most of my classmates. Because my family's Bengali-speaking friends had scattered to suburbs in Long Island and New Jersey, the kids I was closest to in Brooklyn were drawn from a wide range of backgrounds. Though I continued to speak my parents' native language at home, I exclusively spoke English outside of it. True, my family didn't look like the families I saw portrayed on the sitcoms that were practically my religion. Nevertheless, I have never really questioned that I am an American.

But there was a moment in high school when I realized that not all of my peers felt the same way. One day, I was walking to the subway with a classmate, a Bengali-speaking immigrant from India, and we got to talking in Bengali. To my surprise, he rebuked me for the terribleness of my accent, which I falsely believed to be pretty decent, and for having strayed so far from my cultural roots. I don't recall being offended, exactly. He had a point, and I suspect many of my relatives would have agreed with him. I really could have devoted more time and attention to understanding the richness of Bengali culture. Had I been surrounded by more Bengali-speaking immigrants, like my classmate, I probably would have been more culturally Bengali and less culturally American. It just so happens that I came of age before the Bangladeshi and Bengali-speaking Indian communities in and around New York City really mushroomed.

My story is hardly unique. You will likely hear similar stories from millions of other Americans raised in immigrant households. What I am describing is the process of assimilation, in which newcomers and established Americans come to resemble each other. As someone who has gone through this process, you would think I'd be optimistic about the prospects for assimilation in the decades to come. And I am, in a sense. There is no question that, for example, immigrants and their children are mastering the English language.[1]

As my story suggests, though, there is more to assimilation than learning to speak English. In a country as diverse and unequal as ours, not everyone is assimilating into the same America. For Americans growing up in immigrant enclaves, the process of adopting the culture and folkways of the established population is balanced by the pull of the culture of the homeland, which is constantly reinforced by new arrivals.

In the last chapter, I described some of the ways the lives of the descendants of elite immigrants and struggling immigrants diverge. Here I want to focus on the interaction between immigration and group identity, and how it is shaping our political and cultural life.

While some newcomers are being incorporated into the American mainstream—the melting-pot cultural majority forged from the fusion of different ethnic groups—others are being incorporated into disadvantaged groups, which are on average poorer and more vulnerable to negative stereotypes, and that often feel alienated from the mainstream. This is especially true of working-class Hispanic and black newcomers, though other groups are not immune.

The danger, as I see it, is that as the logic of the melting pot fails to take hold, and as more newcomers are incorporated into disadvantaged groups, the level of interethnic tension will skyrocket, to the point where we'll look back wistfully on the halcyon politics of the Trump years. Preventing this nightmare scenario should be our number one priority. Instead, we are sleepwalking right into it.

The Mainstream and the Margins

Throughout our history, Americans have been divided between those who belong to the most powerful and influential cultural group, which I will call the mainstream,[2] and those who belong to disadvantaged groups that find themselves outside of the mainstream. As the sociologist Richard Alba has aptly observed, while the mainstream does not represent American society in its entirety, "it is the part that mistakes itself for the whole."[3] In the early years of the republic, the mainstream consisted of British settlers and their descendants. Over time, though, it came to include a broader universe of people of European descent, as the cultural barriers separating the descendants of settlers and European immigrants started to break down, to the point where they blended together into a broader category of English-speaking whites. This is the classic melting pot that seized the American imagination in the twentieth century. Americans are accustomed to thinking about identity in terms of whites and nonwhites, with whiteness as a stand-in for belonging to the mainstream and nonwhiteness as an indelible mark of outsider status. To make sense of American life, the U.S. Census divides Americans into somewhat arbitrary racial and ethnic categories, which can reinforce the widespread yet false belief that ethnic identity is static, and that the lines separating the majority from various minorities can't really be crossed. The truth is a bit messier. As Alba and others, such as the author Michael Lind,[4] have observed, the melting-pot mainstream is expanding further still, to include a growing number of people whose roots are mostly, if not entirely, non-European.

My own life is a good illustration of how cultural boundaries are blurring. Unlike my parents, who have had to deal with a lot of discrimination over the years, I have been untouched by it. When I have encountered prejudice, it has mostly been of the kind I can safely ignore: from angry drunks, or anonymous lunatics on social media who find the fact that I disagree with them inciting. While I have no doubt that most people have stereotypes in mind when they meet me, based on my appearance and Arabic name, these stereotypes tend to be more positive than negative. For example, because Americans of South Asian descent have a reputation for excelling academically, I suspect many of my teachers and fellow classmates assumed that I'd be a pretty good student when I was younger, which in turn gave me a confidence boost. Had it not been for these positive stereotypes, I honestly don't know how I would have fared. Would I have had the confidence to raise my hand in class, or to think I could thrive at a good college? I doubt it. What I can say with confidence is that my ethnic background hasn't limited me. In that sense, at least, I have assimilated to the American mainstream—not because of any real effort on my part, or because I am a uniquely good or terrible person. In truth, it is mostly a product of circumstances—circumstances that could have been entirely different.

But what about those who haven't been incorporated into the mainstream? Until recently, African Americans were excluded from it, often violently, as were other nonwhite groups. Today, rising rates of intermarriage and residential integration suggest that a growing minority of blacks are finding a place in the mainstream. But it's still just a minority: most blacks, burdened by the legacy of enslavement and segregation, find themselves ghettoized in segregated social networks. Among newcomers of Asian and Latin American origin, we are seeing a range of experiences. In a study of Mexican Americans, Alba, Tomás Jiménez, and Helen Marrow found that at one end of the economic spectrum, Mexican immigrants and their descendants are being incorporated into the mainstream.[5] However, at the other end of it, we're seeing the emergence of (some) Mexican Americans as a marginalized minority, which suffers from persistently low levels of educational attainment and income. While the sheer size of the Mexican-origin population makes its fate particularly important, we see similar dynamics in many other newcomer populations.

So when we talk about assimilation, it is helpful to think of it as a differentiated phenomenon. Drawing on the work of some of the aforementioned scholars, I find it useful to distinguish between *amalgamation*, in which intermarriage and other forms of cultural intermingling cause the ethnic boundaries separating different groups of Americans to blur to the point of insignificance, and *racialization*, in which a minority group finds itself ghettoized in segregated social networks.

Two Immigrants, Two Kinds of Assimilation

Consider the lives of two Spanish-speaking immigrants from Mexico. Patricia is a highly educated bilingual professional who enters the United States on a skilled worker visa, and who works alongside a diverse group of English-speaking colleagues. Influenced by her peers, she settles in a well-off neighborhood, where she meets and eventually marries a second-generation Taiwanese American professional. While Patricia might retain a fondness for all things Mexican, her ethnic origins become less salient over time as she becomes embedded in a decidedly mixed American milieu—a melting pot, in other words. The mixed ancestry of her children has proven an asset, as it has helped them to navigate a variety of different ethnocultural worlds, including the mainstream.

Now imagine Carolina, an immigrant from a less afflu-ent and less educated background, who enters the United States to help out family members living in a working-class Hispanic neighborhood. She, too, meets many Americans, virtually all of whom are Spanish-speaking newcomers much like herself. Carolina forges friendships with Ameri-cans with roots in Mexico, and she eventually marries a second-generation Mexican American whose parents are from her hometown. After a few years in the country, and with the help of her husband, she learns enough English to get by. But as a stay-at-home parent, she doesn't feel all that much pressure to enter the wider English-speaking world. Carolina encourages her husband and her kids to take pride in their Mexicanness and to preserve their ties to their shared homeland. This is partly a defensive measure, as Carolina fears that otherwise her family might take on some of the more destructive aspects of working-class American culture. As her children come of age, they're more American than their mother, and more confidently bilingual. Yet their lives are constrained by the fact that almost all the people they're close to are from their segre-gated ethnic enclave.

As Patricia navigates her mixed neighborhood, most of the mainstream Americans she encounters see her as one of them, not as a member of a separate and distinct group, and so her interactions with them are for the most part friendly and relaxed. She is recognized more for her individual qualities than as a stereotype. Carolina's experience is different. Her growing ethnic enclave abuts a declining neighborhood dominated by older English-speaking Americans who identify with the mainstream, and who increasingly feel outnumbered. In all sorts of subtle ways, Carolina gets the sense that she and her family aren't welcome in certain spaces, which in turn makes her hyperaware of slights and snubs.

And Carolina is not necessarily wrong to think she's being treated unfairly. Our social environment can have a powerful effect on how we perceive other people. Say Patricia is speaking angrily to someone on her phone while walking down the street in her integrated neighborhood. If you see her as an individual, you might assume she is having a rough day and then leave it at that, regardless of her ethnic background, even if you've never met. Now imagine you are a mainstream American living in a community where you feel increasingly outnumbered. Though you consider yourself free of prejudice, you can't help but see Carolina—a stranger—as a member of what you imagine to be her group. And if *she* were to speak angrily on the phone, it might trigger the thought in your mind that *those* people are ill-mannered. Stereotypes of this sort might eventually drive you to move away, which in turn would leave Carolina's neighborhood even more segregated.

Both of these Mexican Americans have assimilated, only in profoundly different ways. Patricia has assimilated into America's melting-pot mainstream. Carolina, meanwhile, has assimilated into America's segregated Hispanic working class. Though Patricia and Carolina are both hardworking people with many praiseworthy qualities, Patricia and her children will have opportunities that Carolina and her children will not.

There is nothing shocking about the fact that educated and affluent immigrants have easier lives than their less fortunate counterparts, or that poorer people live in poorer neighborhoods. And yes, if the only people you know as a poor person are other poor people from similar backgrounds, you might find it somewhat harder to gain access to social and cultural capital that can help you and your loved ones get ahead in life. But is this any reason to be alarmed? The answer is yes.

Why Ethnic Segregation Matters

Why should you care if Carolina's family is living in a segregated enclave, and that mainstream Americans look upon rising ethnic groups with suspicion? Isn't it the case that all immigrant communities fade away and lose their distinctiveness, as has happened time and again in the American past? During the late eighteenth century, for example, it was common for Americans of British descent to fret about the ongoing influx of German-speaking immigrants. Benjamin Franklin warned that if Pennsylvania kept its borders open to them, there was a real danger that the English would one day find themselves Germanized. Thomas Jefferson worried about Germans "settling together in large masses," as that would lead them to "preserve for a long time their own languages, habits, and principles of government." Ridiculous, right? Everyone knows that German Americans were fully incorporated into the English-speaking American mainstream, and that the same has been true of numerous other groups throughout our history.

There is a small wrinkle to the story, though, which is that in the early years of the American republic, immigration levels were low. Most of Europe was engulfed in the Napoleonic Wars, which posed an obstacle to large-scale emigration. The vast majority of the immigrants who made it across the Atlantic were British Protestants, with some German Protestants thrown in. Because most of the newcomers in this era were British, they found it easy, and congenial, to blend in. Moreover, American birthrates were high. In 1800, American women were giving birth to an average of seven children, and though not all of them made it to adulthood, a natural increase was more than enough to ensure a rapidly growing U.S. population. European immigrants were so outnumbered by the native-born descendants of British settlers that you could hardly be blamed for ignoring them. What if American birthrates had been lower, or if the Napoleonic Wars hadn't prevented more German-speaking immigrants from making their way to the fledgling United States? We might instead be talking about Franklin's extraordinary prescience, and you might be reading this book in German. What seems inevitable in hindsight was in reality the product of a set of historical accidents.

When a community of immigrants from a given country is small, and when it is not constantly replenished by new arrivals, it's a safe bet that it will be the immigrants who will be changed by their surroundings. As the years go by, their ties to their homeland will attenuate, and they will tend to blend into the ranks of established Americans. Even if members of a small immigrant community want to wall themselves off from American society, it is hard for them to do so, not least because there is a dearth of young people in the community for their children to befriend and, eventually, to marry. In contrast, when an immigrant community is large, and when it continues to welcome new immigrants from the old country in large numbers, it has a much better shot at remaining separate and distinct, and even of drawing established Americans into its cultural orbit. These immigrants will be changed by living among Americans but their community will have the numbers necessary to maintain a separate existence.

I can speak to this dynamic firsthand. In a funny way, I've been fortunate to be part of an ethnic community that, for now, at least, is pretty small and obscure. Most Americans don't have stereotypes in their heads about

people of Bangladeshi descent, whether positive or negative. When I was growing up, I was one of only a handful of
Bangladeshi Americans in New York City. Between 1980
and 2015, the number of Bangladeshi-born immigrants in
the New York area rose from roughly one thousand to more
than seventy thousand.

Because the Bangladeshi community was so small, my
parents had little choice but to conduct their professional
lives in English, which in turn led to the formation of new
friendships, at least in those early years. My mother worked
in healthcare, where her patients tended to be older native
New Yorkers. She had no choice but to communicate with
them in English, and so she became adept at doing so. For
about a decade, my father was a civil servant by day and an
accountant by night. But in the mid-1990s, state cutbacks
led to the downsizing of his local office, and he was faced
with a choice: he either had to move upstate or leave the
civil service. He decided to leave the civil service to become an accountant full-time. Part of the reason he was
able to make a go of it is that by then, the Bangladeshi population had grown to the point where his native language
skills helped him serve a burgeoning ethnic market. By that
time, I was attending a large, diverse public high school
where I knew two or three Bengali-speakers, and where my
friend network mirrored the composition of the student
body: mostly East Asian and Jewish.

Had I been born thirty years later, in 2009, I would not

have been the only kid of Bangladeshi origin in my kindergarten. Rather, my family would've been part of an established ethnic community, complete with robust religious and cultural institutions. The presence of tens of thousands of other Bangladeshi immigrants would have changed my parents' professional lives, too. They might have entered professional niches dominated by their coethnics, and their fellow Bangladeshis would have provided them with a Bengali-speaking customer base. At the same time, my family would have had fewer interactions with people outside of our ethnic community, and it's far less likely that I'd have had as many friends from different backgrounds.

One of the great truths of immigrant life is that the experience of new immigrants is profoundly shaped by the presence of earlier arrivals with similar skills and backgrounds. Another is that as it grows easier to maintain a connection to your homeland, it can take somewhat longer for those ties to attenuate, and for new relationships and loyalties to take hold.

Granted, there is no reason to believe that the ten millionth immigrant from a given country is any less morally praiseworthy than the first, or the tenth. From a societal perspective, though, there is an important difference between them. Earlier arrivals have little choice but to make their way in the broader community, as there is no ethnic enclave for them to join. Later arrivals, in contrast, have the option of joining, and thus replenishing, already-established ethnic enclaves. In effect, the existence of these enclaves lowers the cost of moving from one country to another. It is one thing to leave behind all that you love and remember from your native country. It is another to know that when you settle in your new country, you will be able to conduct business and forge new relationships with coethnics who share many of your cultural practices and beliefs. This is not to suggest you won't have to change and adapt to your environment. Rather, you won't have to change or adapt quite as much as if you were a lonely pioneer.

And what happens when the cost of migration goes down for the members of a given community? You see more of it. Pioneering immigrants establish themselves, and then they bring family members and friends to join them, whether through formal or informal channels. New York's Bangladeshi community is a good example. Many of the earliest Bangladeshis in Brooklyn were "ship jumpers," i.e., men who worked as deck hands on merchant vessels who literally jumped ship when they arrived on the eastern seaboard.[6] These men then settled in the country as unauthorized immigrants, and some married native-born women, through whom they gained legal status. After doing so, many sponsored family members to join them.

Over time, word of the ship jumpers spread, and they inspired others in their extended networks to make the same journey. Not all Bangladeshis who settled in the United States did so unlawfully. Many others, typically drawn from better-off backgrounds, entered the country as foreign students or as skilled workers, and they, too, encouraged loved ones to make the trek. A major amnesty for unauthorized immigrants in the 1980s allowed many Bangladeshis to become lawful permanent residents, which in turn allowed them to sponsor relatives of their own. Bangladesh's inclusion in the diversity visa lottery program created yet another route through which Bangladeshis could settle in the United States.

In recent years, the once-anodyne term "chain migration" has become contentious, mostly because it's often used by restrictionists calling for limits on family-based admissions. The truth is that family-based admissions are only part of the story of what we might instead call *linked* migration, in which the establishment of an ethnic community draws in not just the relatives of immigrants but also other coethnics looking to better their lives. That's how you go from one thousand to seventy thousand Bangladeshi-born New Yorkers over such a short interval. But even then, seventy thousand Bangladeshi immigrants in a city of 8.5 million is still minuscule. What if the size of the community were far larger?

In short, as the size of a given ethnic group increases, so, too, does in-group contact and interaction, which gives rise to more in-group solidarity. This, in turn, can engender suspicion and resentment from those who don't belong to the group, especially if their groups are stagnant by comparison.

The Risk of Racialization

Of course, this isn't the only possible outcome. Amalgamation is still possible. To achieve it, though, the conditions have to be favorable. Many thoughtful people, such as Richard Alba, believe that the key to amalgamation is robust economic growth.[7] He points to the postwar economic expansion, when rapid economic growth helped European immigrants and their descendants enter the WASP-dominated mainstream. Had growth been less robust, and had native white Protestants perceived immigrant economic gains as a threat to their own prosperity, Alba suggests that there would have been far more interethnic tension. And he makes a compelling case, at least in part. During periods of "non-zero-sum mobility," as he calls it, advantaged groups feel less threatened by disadvantaged groups, and so they are less inclined to protect their privileged position by reinforcing the boundaries that separate them. Alba points to the postwar expansion of public higher education, the role of subsidized homeownership and infrastructure investment in driving suburbanization, and various other social programs as crucial to advancing the economic interests of a pan-ethnic mass middle class, and he wants to see similar efforts today. He sees an analogy to the coming decades, when he anticipates that as younger cohorts take their place in the workforce, the number of non-Hispanic whites available to take on high-wage, high-prestige employment opportunities will fall, and so elites will have no choice but to open up the middle and upper rungs of the labor-force ladder to the historically disadvantaged.

All of this makes sense in principle, and I am sympathetic to Alba's goals. However, ramping up economic growth is easier said than done. To increase average living standards, policymakers would have to promote rapid productivity growth, not just growth in the aggregate size of the economy. There is no straightforward formula for doing so, as evidenced by the fact that productivity growth has been stagnant in virtually all of the world's major market democracies for years. And even if robust productivity growth were within reach, there are a number of other differences between the postwar years and our own time that pose serious obstacles to amalgamation. During an era of high immigration levels, conflicts over immigration and ethnic change tend to divide the working class. As the historian Jefferson Cowie has observed, limits on immigration gave rise to the more unified, and more conformist, culture of midcentury America, which helped set the stage for the New Deal consensus.[8] Had the immigrant replenishment of the early 1900s continued without interruption, it is not at all clear that we'd have seen non-zero-sum mobility in those years. Indeed, one of the least contested findings of recent research on immigration is that it's not natives who bear the brunt of labor market competition with immigrants, but rather immigrants who arrived in the country a bit earlier. That is, new Italian immigrants typically competed with earlier Italian immigrants with similar skills. Had the Italian influx continued without interruption, it is Italian Americans who would have seen their wage growth slow down, or perhaps even go into reverse.

Moreover, the skills gap between low-skill European immigrants and mainstream Americans weren't nearly as pronounced in the 1900s, and so the children of European immigrants didn't have quite as far to climb to enter the middle class as the children of more recent low-skill immigrants. Another difference is that, as we'll discuss in the next chapter, demand for low-skill labor has greatly diminished, thanks in part to the fact that a lot of low-skill work can now be offshored or automated. Low-skill immigrants thus find it hard to escape impoverished enclaves to climb into the pan-ethnic middle class.

How is our current approach raising the risk of racialization? The most obvious example is that for years, we've implicitly tolerated unauthorized immigration, which has arguably been the biggest source of low-skill immigration to the United States in recent decades. Prior to the 1965 immigration reform, migration from source countries in the Western Hemisphere was not subject to numerical limits. Migration flows from Latin America and the Caribbean were only lightly regulated, and so circular migration patterns, in which people traveled back and forth between the United States and their native countries, were fairly common. There was no real expectation that seasonal migrants would integrate into the American mainstream, and the migrant communities that did form were mostly on the margins of American life. After 1965, these migrant networks persisted, but much of the migrant flow from the Americas, and especially from neighboring Mexico, was now unauthorized.

Unauthorized immigration surged from the 1970s through the 1990s, and as the number of unauthorized immigrants increased, so, too, did the intensity of the federal government's border enforcement efforts. Whereas lax enforcement at the border encouraged seasonal migration, tougher border enforcement did the opposite. Rather than risk crossing back and forth, many unauthorized immigrants who found themselves in the United States decided to settle down.[9] Yet by raising the cost of smuggling services, tougher enforcement made unauthorized immigration less attractive to potential migrants from Mexico, especially as the gap in wages for low-skill workers in the United States and Mexico started to shrink. In this sense, border enforcement was somewhat successful, even as it created a large, settled population of unauthorized immigrants.

In response to the unauthorized immigration of this era, Congress passed a series of amnesties from the mid-1980s to the early 1990s that granted large numbers of unauthorized immigrants legal status, thus opening the door to further family-based admissions. At first, the idea was to trade an amnesty for stepped-up interior enforcement, which would deter future unauthorized immigration by making it more difficult for those without authorization to find work. These efforts failed almost entirely, as employer lobbies proved effective at weakening workplace enforcement efforts.[10] The unauthorized immigrant population continued to grow through the 1990s and 2000s. To many immigration restrictionists, the lesson of this experience is painfully clear: the last time we traded amnesty for immigration enforcement, we wound up with amnesty and a surge in unauthorized immigration. It should come as no surprise that restrictionists are skeptical when they are offered the same deal today.

Unauthorized immigration from Mexico has slowed down in recent years, and it may even have gone into reverse. Indeed, some have gone so far as to argue that we're witnessing the end of low-skill immigration to the United States as a result. For example, the economists Gordon Hanson, Chen Liu, and Craig McIntosh, all of the University of California, San Diego, have pointed to the role of demographic changes in Mexico and Central America.[11] Essentially, the Mexican population is aging rapidly, as are populations throughout Latin America. The most drastic change will be in El Salvador, whose population relative to the United States' will decline rapidly, and reach 1980s levels by 2050. Mexico will follow the same pattern but with a slower decline.

The predictions of Hanson, et al, may or may not be borne out. Regardless, the fact remains that the United States is now home to more than ten million unauthorized immigrants, most whom have been living and working in the United States for a decade or more.[12] At this point, most Americans favor granting legal status to the long-resident unauthorized immigrant population.

But until that happens, unauthorized immigrants find themselves caught in a gray area, which makes it exceptionally difficult for them to make meaningful economic progress. Unauthorized immigrants are far more likely to find themselves trapped in segregated enclaves than lawful immigrants, and they and their citizen children are thus more vulnerable to racialization.

To partisans of more open borders, the answer to this problem is simple: we can end unauthorized immigration by getting rid of restrictions entirely, or at least by relaxing limits on low-skill immigration. While I am sympathetic to legalizing long-settled unauthorized immigrants, for reasons I will explain in a later chapter, opening the door to more low-skill immigration would mean the further replenishment of impoverished communities. And replenishment can contribute to racialization as well.

The Intermarrying Kind

Take the contrasting experiences of Mexican Americans, a community that has grown due to immigration over the past forty years, and Italian Americans, a community that has grown much less distinctive over time. Roughly 35 percent of Mexican Americans were born in Mexico, and roughly another third are the U.S.–born children of Mexican immigrants.[13] In contrast, an overwhelming majority of Italian Americans were born in the United States. Jiménez has argued that one of the main differences between the Mexican-origin population in the United States and the white-ethnic descendants of immigrants who arrived in the early 1900s is that mass European immigration ended more than eighty years ago, and so Italian Americans do not generally find themselves in social worlds dominated by recent Italian immigrants.[14] The result is that Italian American identity is largely symbolic and optional, and Italian Americans are perceived as no different from other white Americans. When Italians stopped arriving in America, Italian Americans had little choice but to marry non–Italian Americans. The Mexican American ethnic community, in contrast, was until recently constantly being replenished by new Mexican arrivals, which in turn has sharpened the distinctiveness of Mexican identity. Moreover, just as the end of Italian replenishment lessened the competition facing the Italian immigrants of yesteryear, a slowdown in low-skill immigration from Mexico and Central America might give foreign-born Mexican Americans a modicum of economic breathing room. If Mexican-immigrant replenishment really is ending, as seems possible, amalgamation will soon become more of a possibility for Mexican Americans.

Of course, working-class Mexican Americans will face other obstacles. Incorporation into the mainstream is powerfully influenced by social class. Groups that have lower-than-average levels of educational attainment and income are more vulnerable to racialization, and individuals from disadvantaged groups with higher status are more likely to leave their group identities behind as they enter the mainstream. The economists Brian Duncan and Stephen Trejo studied "ethnic attrition," a phenomenon in which U.S.–born individuals choose not to identify with an ethnic group despite having ancestors who belonged to that group. How does ethnic attrition work? There are many third-generation Americans with at least one Mexican-born grandparent, but only 17 percent of them have three or more grandparents born in Mexico. Virtually all third-generation Americans with three or more Mexican-born grandparents identify as Mexican. In contrast, only 58 percent of those with only one Mexican-born grandparent do the same. More striking still, among third-generation American children with at least one Mexican-born grandparent, those who do not identify as Mexican American stay in school longer than those who do.

It would be one thing if the likelihood of intermarriage were identical for more- and less-educated Hispanics, but that's far from the case. Native-born Hispanic women with a college education are more than three times as likely to be married to whites as native-born Hispanics with less than a high school education.[15] This shouldn't be entirely surprising, as people tend to marry people with similar levels of educational attainment. Assuming these college-educated, native-born Hispanic women are marrying college-educated non-Hispanics, it's quite likely both that their children will be college-educated themselves, and that they'd find themselves in social networks that are more Anglo than Hispanic.

If this pattern persists, Hispanic ethnicity will become more closely associated with disadvantage than it is today. The ranks of white people would continue to grow as the children of whites and upwardly mobile Hispanics come to identify as white. So, too, would the ranks of self-identified Hispanics, who'd tend to be less affluent and educated than those who self-identify as non-Hispanic, and who would thus find themselves locked out of the corridors of power.

Many have pointed to ethnic attrition as an indication that amalgamation is proceeding apace, and that concerns about the racialization of American Hispanics are over-blown. The fact that *some* members of disadvantaged groups are upwardly mobile, living in integrated neighborhoods, and forging close ties, including ties of marriage,[16] with members of more advantaged groups, is indeed encouraging. Yet surely the fact that a larger number of Hispanics find themselves concentrated at the bottom of America's social and economic hierarchies deserves more of our attention. For these Americans, racialization is the most likely outcome.

A more selective, skills-based immigration system wouldn't solve every problem—but it would make the challenges we do face more tractable. For one, it would allow us to concentrate more resources on disadvantaged Americans who face the greatest risk of racialization. So why isn't the idea more widely embraced?

The *Backlash* Paradox

Immerse yourself in pro-immigration literature, from the academy and the mainstream media, and you notice a curious pattern of argument: that uncontrolled immigration patterns have awakened racism and bigotry, but that it's nonetheless best to press forward with the permissive policies that have ostensibly produced this conflict.

Consider the influential academic work, *White Backlash: Immigration, Race, and American Politics*, published in 2015.[17] In chapter after chapter, the sociologists Marisa Abrajano and Zoltan L. Hajnal make a compelling case that America's immigration policies are threatening social cohesion. "Immigration is actually leading to greater divisions and tensions," they say. These tensions "spill over" into the political sphere, inflecting issues like taxes and crime—generating authoritarian impulses among whites, undermining support for the welfare state, and threatening ethnic comity.

The book is a prescient case for alarm about the ways in which rapid demographic change is affecting America's political psyche. The widening racial gap in party identification, in particular, bespeaks "a nation in danger of being driven apart." But even in the face of this trend, the authors never consider paring back the mass immigration policies that brought it about. Instead they hope that diversity will eventually bury ethnic conflict and usher in a more liberal future—though they acknowledge an alternate possibility, where "the racial divide in US party politics expands to a racial chasm, and the prospects for racial conflict swell."

In a similar vein, the political scientists Claire L. Adida, David D. Laitin, and Marie-Anne Valfort likewise identify troubling political implications from existing immigration policies but conclude that immigration must be accelerated regardless.[18] They reviewed statistics on Muslim immigration into a variety of Western countries. Their conclusions were grim: "Europe is creating a class of under-employed immigrants who feel little or no connection with their host societies," they write. This is partly a result of bigotry from ethnic majorities. This exclusion, in turn, slows assimilation and heightens alienation in a vicious cycle. But like virtually all other scholars writing on this question, Adida et al. cannot sanction the clear implication of their work: the rate of immigration ought to be slower so that societies have more time to integrate newcomers. Instead, they argue for staying the course, hoping that more intensive anti-discrimination efforts will cause the cycle of prejudice and alienation to abate.

Over the course of the 2016 election, commentators from across the political spectrum warned that a Donald Trump victory could amount to an "extinction-level event" for the American Republic—a political upheaval so tumultuous that it could smash the foundations of the constitutional order itself. Whether this kind of apocalyptic warning will be vindicated remains to be seen. The Republic is still standing as I write these pages. But it is clear that Trump's ascent to power has added fuel to the forces of outrage and polarization now straining our institutions.

How have we found ourselves in so chaotic a political moment? There has been no shortage of answers—from economic inequality to political correctness to overweening social liberalism of all kinds. But there is no doubt that immigration policy was one of the more potent ingredients of the cocktail. This was Trump's core issue during the primaries; the force that animated his base; the unifying theme of the populist explosion that has transformed politics throughout the Western world.

Much academic and journalistic writing on immigration is defined by what might be called the Backlash Paradox. On the one hand, it is clear to most liberal scholars and journalists that mass immigration has contributed to racism and polarization. On the other, they view slowing the pace of immigration as a callow surrender to bigotry, so the only option is to double down on the status quo and hope that the storm passes—even if this approach risks triggering an "extinction-level event" for open societies. It is almost as though these thinkers believe things have to get worse before they can get better—that traditionalists who worry about the pace of cultural change need to be crushed rather than accommodated, especially when it comes to immigration policy.

What this line of thinking misses, however, is that there is nothing intrinsically racist about adopting an immigration policy that would be less likely to spark a nativist backlash. And until we recognize that, our politics will only get uglier.

CHAPTER FOUR

Jobs Robots Will Do

As a professional in New York City, I lead a comfortable life. I can choose from hundreds of restaurants so close to my apartment that my wife could convey me to dinner by piggyback if, say, I beat her at Scrabble. If I'd prefer not to leave home, I can have food delivered and extend a cash-stuffed fist out a crack in my front door, and receive food in return without even having to put on trousers. When I'm running late, I can hail a taxi, whether by raising my hand or tapping my smartphone. Need a dog walker? A cut-rate manicure? A cleaning service to sort through my filth? Done. I am one of the most pampered people to have ever walked the earth. You might be, too.

This all feels strange. Though I grew up in a solidly middle-class family, eating out was a rare treat. If my parents couldn't cook for me, I'd heat up a frozen meal or a can of soup for myself. The thought of hiring a housekeeper would have struck my family as absurdly extravagant. I assumed that only the obscenely rich were in a position to hire help. My parents grew up with servants in their native Bangladesh, which made sense. Bangladesh was one of the world's poorest countries, and even modestly well-off families often had multiple servants, at least until the country's garment industry started to give low-skill workers from the countryside a better option. But in the America of my youthful imagination, hired help seemed like an anachronism.

How did a Salam come to enjoy the lifestyle of a Rockefeller? New York is home to large numbers of people who are willing, if not desperate, to work for low wages. Moreover, as technology continues to advance, people like me will soon be able to access these and other services through a combination of automation and offshoring, which could leave us with a large and growing number of displaced workers. And if these people do indeed lose their jobs, or find their wages squeezed, the more fortunate among us will be responsible for their well-being.

Conventional arguments for and against immigration tend to focus on its immediate costs and benefits. They neglect the many ways immigration can affect the structure of an economy over time, and how changing the composition of the labor force can create new and lasting obligations. Worse still, they glide past the accelerating pace of technological change and the role of offshoring and automation as substitutes for low-skill immigrant labor. In this chapter, I offer a broader look at the economics of immigration, with an emphasis on the fact that modern economies are more fluid than fixed.

Between Sweden and Singapore

The classic argument for low-skill immigration is that low-skill immigrants "do the jobs Americans won't do," and that without them, Americans would see their living standards greatly reduced. Leave aside for the moment that this takes for granted that it is right and proper to treat foreign-born workers as second-class citizens, an assumption I strongly reject, and ignores the question of what happens when immigrants become Americans themselves. There is an obvious lacuna in this line of argument, which is that in a dynamic market economy, employers can always change the way they do business.

Whereas people once had to live in the same cities or at least the same countries to collaborate, that is no longer true. Many of the benefits traditionally associated with low-skill immigration can now be captured through offshoring;

and in the future, virtual presence technology will surely give rise to "virtual immigration," in which foreign workers telecommute to factories, offices, and even homes in affluent countries.[1] At the same time, the accelerating pace of automation has the potential to greatly increase labor productivity, which in turn could reduce our reliance on low-skill labor. These developments won't render low-skill immigration obsolete, but they will give the citizens of desirable destination countries like America the wherewithal to be more selective when it comes to immigration. And we don't have to look to the future to realize that we can do with less low-skill labor. All we have to do is look abroad. Consider, for example, Sweden and Singapore, two of the world's richest, most admired countries.

Sweden has been struggling with the question of how to put low-skill refugees to work. Employment rates for refugees are dismally low, despite the fact that the Swedish government has devoted considerable resources to providing them with language instruction and a wide array of social services. The main challenge is that because Sweden is one of the world's most well-educated societies, its employers have learned to do without a large number of low-wage, low-skill workers.[2] Rather, Swedish business models have been designed to make use of high-skilled, high-wage workers augmented by loads of laborsaving technology. They haven't quite figured out what to do with newly available refugee labor. A further obstacle is that Sweden has a high effective minimum wage, which makes low-skill labor even less attractive.

While Sweden's rigid labor market has done an excellent job of fostering greater equality among native-born Swedes, it has shockingly high unemployment rates among foreign-born workers. In 2017, *The Economist* reported that only half of foreign-born workers who had been in the country for nine years had a job, and the unemployment rates of the foreign-born were still higher than those of the native-born even after twenty years in the country.[3] To put low-skill refugees to work, the Swedish labor market has had to adapt. Some Swedish firms are "de-engineering" their business models to become more labor-intensive. The Swedish government, meanwhile, has moved to slash benefits for immigrants, on the grounds that the arrival of hundreds of thousands of refugees has strained its ability to be as generous as it had been in the past.[4] Swedes of a libertarian bent have welcomed the new openness to low-skill labor. The question is whether most Swedes are eager to embrace a two-tiered labor market, in which an underclass of low-skill immigrants does work that was previously done satisfactorily by a combination of better-paid workers and machines. The evidence suggests not: populists have gained support, and they have done so primarily by promising tighter immigration policies.

While Sweden is trying to nudge its employers to adopt more labor-intensive business models, Singapore is doing the opposite.[5] Like Sweden, Singapore is one of the world's richest countries, and its citizens are also among the best educated in the world. Yet the city-state also makes use of a great deal of low-skill labor via its massive guest-worker program. Rather than taking in refugees, Singapore takes in hundreds of thousands of temporary labor migrants, who drive its taxis, unclog its toilets, and dig its tunnels. Singapore's government rigorously enforces its immigration laws, and temporary labor migrants are truly temporary. There is zero expectation that these migrants will one day be welcomed into citizenship, unless they belong to the ultra-elite minority of highly educated expats. Whereas the Swedes are committed to spending generously on refugees and other poor migrants, in the hope of fully integrating them into Swedish society, Singapore takes a less sentimental approach: you are here to work, and once we have gotten what we want out of you, we will ship you back home. (Indeed, Singapore deports low-skill migrant workers who become pregnant.[6])

A few years ago, however, there was a political backlash against Singapore's reliance on foreign-born labor, especially mid-skilled labor in the service sector, which competed more directly with Singaporean natives. The government moved to reduce immigration levels.[7] Recognizing that doing so would squeeze labor-intensive businesses, however, the Singaporean government struck a bargain with employers: hire more Singaporean natives, and in return we'll pay you to adopt laborsaving technologies that will reduce your cost of doing business over time. Many of Singapore's low-wage employers have resisted the new policies, as they have grown accustomed to relying on guest workers. Others, however, have been delighted by the resulting efficiency gains.

It is not America's style to approach its labor market challenges so systematically. The United States has done a far better job of incorporating its large pool of low-skill immigrant workers than Sweden, thanks in large part to low minimum wages and a lightly regulated labor market. The United States has also largely eschewed Singapore's solution of actively encouraging firms to economize on low-wage labor, presumably because Americans are allergic to Singapore-style central planning. Yet relying on low-skill immigration is a choice, not a necessity. And it is not the wisest choice, either.

The Short Run and the Long Run

We should distinguish between how immigration affects the labor market in the short run and in the long run.

First, imagine that there are only two kinds of workers, high-skill and low-skill. Second, let's stipulate that while the business models used by employers to produce goods and provide services are fixed in the short run, employers can develop new business models in the long run.

What does it mean to develop a new business model?

When gas prices start to climb, consumers might respond by driving less, depending on how high prices have gone and how much control they have over their commutes. But they won't replace Hummers with Priuses straightaway. They will wait to see if higher gas prices persist. Alternatively, if gas prices plummet, and then plateau at a low level, we can expect consumers to drive more, and to start giving gas-guzzlers a long look. The important thing to understand is that this adjustment process does not happen instantaneously.

Something similar happens when there is a shock to the supply of labor. Say there is a huge and sudden influx of immigrants, and that the new arrivals are mostly low-skill. It makes intuitive sense that in the short run, at least, the increased supply of low-skill immigrant workers will drive down wages for low-skill native workers. Over the long run, though, employers can adapt to the increased supply of low-skill workers by adopting more labor-intensive business models. Why rely on expensive machines to do work that can be done more cost-effectively by hand, thanks to all of the low-skill labor that is available? In a few years' time, the adoption of more labor-intensive business models can turn what was once a surplus of low-skill labor into a shortage, at which point wages start going up.

What would happen if most of the arrivals were high-skill? In that case, employers would eventually find a way to make use of them, and incumbent low-skill workers might benefit, as they would complement the newcomers. And what if the immigrant influx perfectly mirrored the existing population in terms of skill? In that case, the economy would look pretty much the same, only it would be commensurately bigger in scale.[8]

Most immigration skeptics focus on the possibility that the arrival of new immigrants will drive down the wages of natives with similar skills. That is clearly bad news for said natives. Let's not forget, though, that if immigrants drive down wages, they also drive down the price of labor-intensive goods and services consumed by everyone, including natives. The bigger the negative impact of immigration on native wages, the bigger the positive impact on consumer prices. As a general rule, the biggest beneficiaries of immigration are the immigrants themselves. They are the ones who move from one country to another for a better life, and they are the ones who are presumably earning higher wages than they would have otherwise. The chief benefit to natives comes in the form of lower prices. The more immigrant workers drive down wages, the bigger the overall immigration surplus that accrues to natives.

Immigration's actual impact on wages is one of the most hotly contested claims in economics. Leading economists have found that the impact of immigration on native wages has, in fact, been very modest—and indeed, that it has been modestly positive.[9] Pessimists claim that immigration has slightly reduced the wages of low-skill natives. Even so, the most widely cited pessimists acknowledge that low-skill immigration has increased the wages of high-skill natives, because low-skill immigrants complement high-skill natives, for example, the availability of a low-skill immigrant caregiver can allow a high-skill, native-born parent to work longer hours as a high-wage professional. Optimists claim that immigration has increased the wages of *all* natives, including low-skill natives, while only lowering the wages of *previous* immigrants. The funny thing is that the differences here aren't all that great. Immigration has either raised wages by an extremely small amount or it has lowered them by an extremely small amount. Either way, wages are not the central issue.

How Offshoring Changes the Immigration Debate

If immigration doesn't necessarily drive down native wages, what exactly is the problem? Why not take a page from Singapore and expand low-wage guest-worker programs? If we are worried about the welfare costs, we could explicitly bar those who sign up for them from ever receiving safety-net benefits, as in the monogenerational immigration systems we discussed earlier. One reason we can't do that, which I alluded to earlier, is that many of us find the idea of a permanent underclass of low-wage workers disturbing and undemocratic. Perhaps this objection would be moot if low-skill immigration were the only way for American households to capture the benefits of low-skill labor. But there are, in fact, other ways to profit from the availability of low-skill labor. For one, U.S. consumers are free to purchase labor-intensive goods and services from abroad. The historical decline of protectionism has made restricting low-skill immigration a more viable option. Thanks to offshoring, it is possible to pursue greater egalitarianism at home while providing employment opportunities for low-wage workers abroad.

Take the case of South Korea, which has gone from being one of the world's poorest countries to one of its richest in the space of a few decades. One of the reasons South Korea has grown so rich is that it has a highly educated population and it has not hesitated to embrace productivity-boosting automation. Rather than rely on low-skill immigrants, Korean businesses thrive by making greater use of industrial robots and other laborsaving technologies, and by partnering with employers in other countries, such as Vietnam. In recent years, Samsung, one of South Korea's most storied multinationals, has invested $17 billion in Vietnam, where its local subsidiary now employs over 100,000 people.[10] In theory, South Korea could have admitted 100,000 Vietnamese immigrants to its shores, where they would do the exact same jobs for slightly higher wages. However, doing so would have caused enormous disruption in the lives of these Vietnamese workers and, at the same time, it would have made South Korea a far more unequal society. Instead, workers in South Korea and Vietnam are collaborating in ways that allow the former country to remain relatively egalitarian while making Vietnam far more productive and affluent than it would have been in the absence of South Korean investment. A devoted cosmopolitan might fault South Korea's voters for not being enlightened enough to welcome the prospect of admitting lots of Vietnamese workers, but the deepening of economic ties between South Korea and Vietnam seems to be working out rather well for all concerned, even without mass migration.

This example might strike you as counterintuitive. It often seems as though protectionism and immigration restriction are a package deal. And as a matter of cultural sensibilities, they do tend to go together. Simply put, the kind of people who celebrate free trade tend to be the kind of people who have a taste for change, which makes them more favorably disposed toward the free movement of people across borders.[11] Similarly, on the other side of the political fence, immigration skeptics are often motivated by a sense of nostalgia, which inclines them to oppose offshoring, automation, and other forces that threaten to change the look and feel of society.

In practice, though, offshoring enables large U.S. employers to substitute low-skill workers abroad for low-skill workers at home. This is in stark contrast to the first decades of the twentieth century, when the rise of American industry was fueled by low-skill immigrant labor. But now, it's possible to contract out the most labor-intensive parts of production to firms and workers based in countries where low-skill labor is cheap and labor standards are lax, or to adopt capital-intensive business models that use low-skill labor sparingly, if at all. The result is that tradable sector employment in the United States is increasingly skewed toward high-skill workers, who work in tandem with low-skill labor overseas. Meanwhile, low-skill workers in the United States typically find themselves employed by smaller, lower-productivity firms that pay lower wages, with business models that likely wouldn't survive years of serious, sustained wage gains.

Inevitably, this changing economic landscape has influenced the politics of low-skill immigration. In *Trading Barriers*, the UCLA political scientist Margaret E. Peters finds that as barriers to trade have fallen, barriers to low-skill immigration have risen.[12] While others have argued that restrictionism has gained ground because nativism is on the march, or because the expansion of the welfare state has intensified concerns about the fiscal impact of low-skill immigration, Peters offers a novel and quite compelling explanation that has been hitherto neglected, namely, that major corporations have lost their appetite for using their considerable resources to fight the restrictionist tide.

There are plenty of corporations that celebrate immigration-driven cultural change and diversity, and of course corporate America still lobbies aggressively for openness to *high*-skill immigration. Low-skill immigration is a different story. Though it remains essential to sustaining the low-skill workforce in the United States, as rising educational attainment and falling birthrates would otherwise cause it to shrink over time, the fact that firms can simply import labor-intensive intermediate inputs rather than produce them in-house has made the availability of low-skill labor a less urgent, if not superfluous, concern.

As corporate demand for low-skill labor has fallen, corporate lobbying for low-skill immigration has fallen off. This in turn has changed the character of immigration advocacy, reducing its emphasis on the priorities of low-wage employers, such as the creation and expansion of guest-worker programs, and increasing its emphasis on the rights of immigrants to reunite with their family members—and, in intellectual circles, on immigration as a vehicle for the uplift of the global poor. Peters, for instance, concludes her book by offering a moral defense of open borders.

Mind you, economic self-interest still plays a role in the coalition for low-skill immigration: affluent professionals, for example, greatly benefit from an abundance of low-skill immigrant labor, as it makes it cheaper for them to outsource household production. At the same time, affluent professionals are potentially disadvantaged by the arrival of high-skill immigrants capable of competing with them for high-wage, high-status jobs. A widely cited study by the economists Patricia Cortés and José Tessada found that "the immigration wave of 1980 to 2000 increased by close to twenty minutes a week the amount of time women at the top quartile of the wage distribution devote to market work," and that it saved women working in the most demanding professions about seven minutes a week of household work.[13] Needless to say, an extra seven minutes can make an enormous difference in one's life. Regardless, self-interested arguments increasingly play second fiddle to more emotionally resonant appeals centered on the moral worthiness of immigrants themselves, and for good reason: the argument for economic self-interest is, if anything, growing weaker over time.

The Cosmopolitan Case for Robophobia

Though offshoring can serve as a substitute for low-skill immigration, the reverse can also be true. At high enough levels of low-skill immigration, it is certainly possible that U.S. firms would find it more profitable to bring the most labor-intensive parts of production back home, particularly if the United States were to abolish the minimum wage and other regulations that raise the cost of low-skill labor. Under these circumstances, it's not just offshoring that might go into reverse. The same could happen to laborsaving technologies of all sorts.

Think back to the relationship between gas prices and the prevalence of gas-guzzling cars. If low-skill labor were sufficiently abundant, no one would bother to work on self-driving cars and delivery drones, as chauffeurs and bicycle messengers could be had at cut-rate prices. Indeed, in the absence of low-skill immigration, many of today's low-wage jobs—in agriculture, garment manufacturing, meatpacking, and retail—would *already* be done by machines or by workers overseas.

Consider the case made by Lant Pritchett, a senior fellow at the Center for Global Development and a leading advocate of open borders immigration policies. He notes that low-skill labor is one of the world's most abundant economic resources, and that the United States could easily increase its supply of it. Beyond the domestic labor force, there should be plenty of foreign workers ready to settle here as well. By his count, there are a billion people between the ages of fifteen to forty-nine whose skills earn them less than $5,000 a year at home, corrected for purchasing power, but who could make more than $20,000 in the United States.[14] In other words, the United States' potential low-skill labor pool is vast.

So why, Pritchett asks, are the country's brightest minds focused on finding ways to take human workers out of the equation? Think of the billions that have gone into driverless cars, automated checkout processes in the grocery store, and, perhaps eventually, deliveries by drone. At first glance, these projects make little economic sense. With labor as abundant as it is, it should be very cheap. Forget about leaving a $5,000-a-year job for a $20,000 one. Pritchett suggests that a 50 or 100 percent wage premium should be enough to convince a worker from a developing country to leave home.[15]

Why, then, hire best-in-class U.S. researchers and dump billions into R&D to build a robot when you could just hire cheaper foreign labor to do the job manually? Is it that America's tech firms are foolish and wasteful? Not at all. It makes perfectly good business sense for them to do so, on the grounds that U.S. immigration policies are, according to Pritchett, needlessly tight. Amazon's quest to hire expensive MIT engineers to work on robotics is thus instructive. The company does so, "at least in part, because Amazon's labor costs—including the difficulty of reliably filling jobs, turnover, wages, benefits, etc.—are high. But those labor costs *overestimate* the true economic scarcity of labor to the U.S. economy by a *factor of four* due entirely to border based barriers to mobility of labor."[16]

Pritchett deserves a great deal of credit for making his case so plainly. It is worth noting, however, that labor scarcity has been a boon to innovation for centuries. Robert Allen, an economic historian at Oxford, has argued that the Industrial Revolution itself represented a creative response to a scarce supply of labor.[17] By the 1700s, England already dominated the Europe-wide market for wool textiles, and

the expansion of its influence in Asia and the Americas created new markets for its wares. To meet rising global demand, local firms hired workers from the countryside at a
furious pace. At first, wage pressures were slight, as there
was a seemingly inexhaustible number of farmers to be re-
cruited. Over time, though, the balance started to shift: the
population of the cities grew while the population of the
countryside fell, to the point where good workers were hard
to find. It's at this point that clever inventors and entrepreneurs dreamed up new laborsaving technologies that could
give them an edge over their competitors. Though these
technologies weren't all that useful outside of England in the
early years, English industrialists gradually perfected them
until they become useful in other countries, where labor
was cheaper. And that's how the Industrial Revolution
spread. Now imagine what would have happened if English
employers had access to a truly inexhaustible supply of labor. It is possible that humanity might never have escaped its
impoverished pre-industrial state.

Closer to home, labor scarcity has been the historical se-
cret to America's prosperity. Why did American industry
devise so many laborsaving technologies, such as inter-
changeable parts and the assembly line? Unlike in hide-
bound Europe, where employers had enjoyed access to a
captive and comparatively low-cost source of labor, free
American workers had the escape valve of the frontier, and
so industrialists had little choice but to pay higher wages.

Manufacturers responded by economizing on the scarce labor supply by dreaming up new ways of doing business. Immigration has helped ease America's labor scarcity. For most of American history, however, the high cost and arduousness of the journey to the United States limited the number who could make it. Never have our immigration levels come close to what we'd see if all barriers to the mobility of labor were lifted tomorrow.

Yet it must be said that the world Pritchett describes could have real benefits for native-born workers, especially those who long for managerial roles. Recall our discussion of Qatar, where 94 percent of the workforce is foreign-born. Native-born Qatari citizens don't ordinarily see low-wage guest workers as competitors. Rather, they see them as helpmates, who pose no threat to their elevated social status. Similarly, if the United States were to drastically increase low-skill immigration, new arrivals wouldn't simply crowd out native workers. By forestalling automation, entire sectors that would otherwise vanish would continue to exist, and these sectors would undoubtedly employ natives.

Take the case of the end of the *bracero* program in 1965, the subject of a paper by the economists Michael Clemens, Ethan Lewis, and Hannah Postel.[18] Between 1942 and 1965, the U.S. and Mexican governments agreed to allow Mexican seasonal workers to take jobs on U.S. farms. Congress voted to end the *bracero* program in part out of a desire to raise wages for U.S. farmworkers. What they failed to appreciate is that rather than raise wages in a sustained fashion, farmers had an alternative: they could adopt existing mechanical harvest technologies that would greatly reduce their reliance on human labor, and they could devise entirely new production techniques that would do the same. Sure enough, that's what happened. Labor scarcity didn't result in farmworkers raising their incomes. Rather, it resulted in fewer farmworkers. And there's evidence that in immigrant-rich regions of the United States, a similar dynamic is at work in a number of different sectors: mechanization and automation is slower in these regions relative to regions where immigrants are scarce.[19]

To many low-skill immigration advocates, the takeaway from the findings of Clemens et al. is clear: immigration restriction is foolish, as it will only accelerate job destruction. There is another way to look at it, however: once the *bracero* program ended, farmers adopted readily available technologies that increased their productivity; U.S. farmworkers were displaced in the process, which was presumably painful, but over time they and their descendants have found employment in other sectors. Sustaining high levels of agricultural employment is beneficial to farmworkers, and especially to those who are risk-averse and disinclined to change their jobs or to move. From a societal perspective, though, it is not clear that we should lament the reallocation of workers from a low-wage, low-productivity sector to rising sectors. Indeed, this process has been the chief driver of rising productivity and prosperity throughout American history.

While it would be ungenerous to describe open borders advocates as Luddites—Pritchett, for one, explicitly rejects the label—it does make sense for them to make common cause with those who fear that technological progress will destroy the jobs of low-skill natives. It appears to be true that in regions that attract large numbers of low-skill immigrants, low-skill immigrants take low-wage manual jobs while low-skill natives find themselves a step above them. And if an even greater abundance of low-skill immigrant labor made hand-drawn rickshaws a viable alternative to automobiles, we can expect that there would be native-born, English-speaking dispatchers further up the chain of command.

Should we welcome a future in which low-skill U.S. citizens serve as the superintendents of vast armies of low-skill guest-workers, who would do work with their hands that is now done by machines or in the teeming factories of the developing world? Many immigration advocates would insist that the answer is yes. Along these lines, Glen Weyl and Eric Posner have proposed an ingenious "Visas Between Individuals Program"[20] that would allow all U.S. citizens to sponsor economic migrants, whom they could charge a substantial fee—and toward whom they might feel a sense of paternalistic obligation. It is an intriguingly inegalitarian vision that brings to mind the liberal imperialism of yesteryear.

There are a few sticking points, however. The first and most obvious is that a program like the one Weyl and Posner envision would have profound consequences for political equality, as they would readily acknowledge. In the past, Weyl and Posner have called for mass guest-worker programs precisely because they recognize that U.S. citizens are reluctant to open the doors to citizenship to all potential migrants.[21] And so they see a system of temporary labor visas as a way to give the global poor access to the U.S. labor market without also granting them full membership in the American polity. Though we already do this on a small scale, guest-worker programs that would welcome tens of millions would create new cleavages in our society.

Assume for the moment that our main motivation for increasing low-skill immigration were to improve the relative status of low-skill natives, on the grounds that we don't want low-skill natives to have to take on low-wage manual jobs. We'd much rather they be the bosses of low-wage immigrant laborers, which would ensure that they'd be in the middle rather than the bottom of the income distribution. This is certainly an interesting position to take, but we could also improve the well-being of low-skill natives by, say, encouraging them to upgrade their skills, or by subsidizing their wages. Increasing low-skilled immigration is hardly the most straightforward way to help them.

Of course, helping low-skill natives needn't be our objective. Say we were to open our borders, with an eye toward driving down wages for low-skill work in the United States while raising the living standards of some of the world's poorest people, the idea being that this would be a win-win policy—good for U.S. consumers and good for fighting poverty. Many Americans might worry that workers earning, say, $15,000 a year would find it difficult to afford dignified lives in the United States, or that the arrival of tens of millions of low-wage workers would change the character of their communities. Open borders advocates would reply that the first objection is absurd, because the migrants in question are presumably better off than they would have been otherwise, and that the second is racist or (more politely) xenophobic, as racism and xenophobia are the only possible justification for the mass exclusion of vast numbers of low-wage workers, who'd otherwise build their lives in sprawling favelas ringing every American city. And besides, as long as the foreign workers are granted only temporary labor visas, they can be excluded from the admittedly expensive benefits of full membership in society.

Nevertheless, it is still not clear that it would be preferable to have a low-wage worker do a job that could be done just as easily—and just as inexpensively, at least in time—by a machine. There may well be a powerful moral case that wealthy Americans ought to replace their air-conditioning units with a rotating cast of earnest young people who would be willing to fan them around the clock. Yet it is hard to deny that doing so would be rather inconvenient. Instead of a win-win, this approach seems more like a win for low-skill immigrants and a mixed bag at best for consumers who would be just as content with technological alternatives to low-skill labor—not to mention that such an arrangement would lead to the death of any kind of civic solidarity.

Moreover, if our objective is to stymie the development and adoption of laborsaving technologies, a unilateral decision on the part of the United States to open its borders wouldn't be nearly enough. We would have to ensure that, for example, rapidly aging societies in East Asia were committed to doing the same. Otherwise, entrepreneurs and inventors in China and Japan might pioneer technologies and business models that have the potential to spread beyond their borders—a development that is not entirely hypothetical.

The Rocky Road to Robotopia

Aren't there innumerable low-skill jobs that are simply not substitutable? Sluggish labor force growth in the United States means that we can't come close to filling them without welcoming low-skill immigrants. At times, one hears a corollary argument, namely, that an alarmingly high proportion of low-skill U.S. natives are ill-suited to doing difficult and dangerous jobs that simply need to be done. We don't have to indulge crazy fantasies about hand-drawn rickshaws or foreigners fanning wealthy Americans. Who is going to pick the fruit? And who is going to clear the bedpans?

In 2012, the immigration researchers Frank Bean, Susan Brown, James Bachmeier, Zoya Gubernskaya, and Christopher Smith identified a number of reasons low-wage employers might prefer low-skill immigrants to low-skill natives, which were ably summarized by the conservative policy analyst James Pethokoukis[22] of the American Enterprise Institute: First, whereas low-skill natives are often reluctant to move from their hometowns to opportunity-rich locales, low-skill immigrants have already made that leap, and so they're naturally more likely to be willing to move within the United States. Second, low-skill natives are more likely to struggle with alcohol and drug abuse than their foreign-born counterparts, a self-selecting population of strivers. Relatedly, low-skill natives are more likely to report being in worse health than low-skill immigrants. And finally, low-skill natives are more likely to be ex-offenders than low-skill immigrants. Bean et al. acknowledge the possibility that automation and offshoring might diminish the number of low-skill job openings in the years to come, but they expect the impact to be minimal.

There is something more than a little circular about their line of argument. Consider the supposed unfitness of low-skill natives. While it is undoubtedly true that many have been scarred by the lingering effects of childhood poverty, there is considerable evidence that many of the social maladies associated with unemployment and underemployment can be cured, or at least greatly mitigated, by a tight labor market.

Arthur Okun, one of the founding fathers of modern macroeconomics, popularized the term "high-pressure economy" to refer to a state of affairs in which unemployment is low and overall economic growth is high.[23] Workers who might struggle to find remunerative employment in a low-pressure economy, where the opposite conditions prevail, thrive in a high-pressure economy, when employers have little choice but to invest in improving their production techniques and providing all of their workers with the capital they need to increase output. At the start of the 2017 tourist season, for example, restaurants and resorts in coastal Maine started hiring furloughed ex-offenders to keep up with demand.[24] Eventually, employers might have no choice but to invest more in training low-skill workers, in the hopes of boosting their productivity levels. Judging by past experiences, they'll invest in training only as a last resort. But they'll get there.

And in time, a high-pressure economy tends to accelerate technological progress. It is only when low-wage workers start quitting their jobs to take better jobs offering higher pay that their employers will break a sweat trying to replace them. In California, a shortage of low-wage immigrant workers in the agricultural sector has set off a mad scramble among entrepreneurs and technologists to devise new laborsaving technologies, and it has led farmers to shift from labor-intensive crops such as grapes and asparagus to almonds, which are easier to harvest by machine—a scramble reminiscent of the one that followed the end of the *bracero* program.[25]

But again, aren't there jobs that will always be with us, irrespective of the tightness of the labor market? Consider a few classic examples of supposedly nonsubstitutable jobs: Custodial services have long been insulated from offshoring, and it is hard to imagine an America bereft of janitors, yet already we're seeing robotic vacuums and mops capable of doing industrial jobs. And in the future, we can expect that buildings will be reconfigured and materials will be selected to make them more tractable for robotic cleaning devices. No doubt new cleaning systems will require specialized human workers to operate and maintain them, but it is unlikely we will need quite as many of them as we do today. Furthermore, much of the work of operating and maintaining these devices can be done remotely, a subject to which I'll return.

What about home health aides, an occupation that is growing enormously as the U.S. population ages? This is an area where productivity increases will be difficult to achieve, not least because of the fragmentation among U.S. medical providers. Yet here, too, there are opportunities for automation, as seen with the advent of machines capable of administering sedatives to elderly patients and robot bellhops that can help meet the basic needs of nursing-home patrons. The number of truly nonsubstitutable low-skill jobs is almost certainly smaller than Bean et al. anticipate.

Perhaps I haven't convinced you that janitors and home health aides will one day be middle-class professionals who find themselves augmented by a slew of sophisticated technologies. Fair enough. There really are reasons to believe some jobs aren't going away: this is particularly true in sectors that are stringently regulated, such as medical care, where the doctors' lobby can be expected to fight business models that might reduce the pay or prestige of physicians, or where there is intense cultural resistance to automation, such as child care. But even if we accept that there are millions of low-skill jobs that will need to be filled in the decades to come, why would we assume that only low-skill workers would be willing to take them on? Labor scarcity could lead to higher wages, which would in turn attract domestic workers. While this might seem as though it would be cripplingly expensive, remember that we are talking about nonsubstitutable jobs. Other sectors will presumably have seen large productivity gains, which would create new wealth that could then flow to workers in the nonsubstitutable jobs that remain.

And we shouldn't neglect the possibility that the automation of *high*-skill jobs might expand the labor pool available to take on non-routine manual tasks that, for now, only humans can perform. As John Horton, a labor economist at NYU, has argued,[26] most low-skill jobs in the United States and other rich market democracies are high-touch jobs in the service sector that, in their current form, require a degree of emotional intelligence that machines can't match. This is one of the stronger arguments for the proposition that low-skill jobs will always be with us, and there's some evidence for it. For example, as the number of ATMs has soared, retail banks have hired more bank tellers and greeters to improve their customer experience. As a general rule, these jobs are not very well-compensated for the simple reason that they don't require much in the way of specialized training, which means that there are many people who can do them. Because these jobs don't pay terribly well, there's not much of a burning desire to automate them out of existence.

However, the same can't be said for highly specialized jobs that require a great deal of expensive training, taken up by employees who can be choosy about where they work. It is these footloose, expensive, specialized workers whom employers are keen to replace, and the good news for employers is that artificial intelligence is potentially very well-suited to taking on many specialized tasks. Horton cites accountants and auditors as the kind of workers who are especially vulnerable to advances in AI. Whereas a truck driver displaced by self-driving technology might find it relatively easy to become a maintenance worker or even a construction laborer with a bit of retraining, an accountant or auditor can't easily become a nurse practitioner or a software developer, two jobs that at the moment are similarly well-compensated and prestigious.

If Horton is right, many accountants and auditors will either be in for a long and arduous process of clawing their way back into the skilled middle class or they will have no choice but to further swell the ranks of the low-wage workforce, working in jobs that pay too little to make automation worthwhile. If this were indeed to happen, it would represent a massive social challenge, as large numbers of Americans would find themselves earning less than they had hoped. The political scientist Darrell M. West, drawing on a range of studies, warns that the social consequences of automation could be dire.[27] "If the employment impact falls at the 38 percent mean of these forecasts," he warns, "Western democracies likely could resort to authoritarianism as happened to some countries during the Great Depression of the 1930s in order to keep their restive populations in check."

Under these circumstances, it is hard to imagine that a large increase in low-skill immigration would be welcome. In fact, I would argue that much of today's anti-immigration backlash stems from the fact that we have already botched a similarly wrenching transition—the transition to a more globalized economy.

Are We Doomed to Repeat the Globalization Backlash?

With my having praised the benefits of offshoring, you might assume that I am a fan of globalization. And you'd be right. Globalization has been a boon to many Americans, especially those wealthy enough to own stock in U.S. companies and those working in senior management. And, of course, it is not just the rich who have benefited. Ordinary consumers have reaped the benefit of higher-quality, lower-cost goods, which have helped improve living standards despite years of sluggish wage growth. Similarly, landlords and service workers in cities full of professionals in globalized industries—such as San Francisco, New York, and Washington, DC—have benefited, too. Most students of globalization's impact on the U.S. economy would argue that in aggregate terms, these benefits have outweighed the costs.

But that is not to say that the costs haven't been high. On the other side of the ledger, millions of U.S. workers have found it difficult, if not impossible, to compete with Chinese labor. Who are the workers who've found it most difficult to adapt to the new global division of labor? It's mostly older low-skill workers employed in manufacturing and, more broadly, workers in manufacturing-heavy regions. When the local factory closes, it impacts not just local factory workers but also the workers at local restaurants and retailers, and the public employees who are kept afloat by local tax revenue.

To say that the transition to a more globalized economy has been rocky would be an understatement. Globalization's impact on the Rust Belt has sapped confidence in the basic fairness of America's institutions, and it has engendered an intense political backlash. That's why policymakers are so interested in the question of how we should have adapted to globalization, and what we can realistically do now to ensure that its benefits are spread more broadly.

One answer is that we could have helped workers displaced from the tradable sector in depressed communities—think manufacturing workers who lost out from competing with Chinese imports—find new employment in the nontradable sector in thriving communities—e.g., construction workers or nurses in globalization's new boomtowns. This might have meant investing more in displaced workers by offering more in the way of retraining (to help them gain new skills), wage subsidies (to ease the burden of taking on lower-paid jobs), and relocation assistance (to help them move to regions with stronger labor markets).

But for this strategy to work, you would need there to be

employers willing to retrain older Rust Belt workers, and an abundant supply of affordable housing in the same cities and towns where there is an abundant supply of jobs. Society would have had to change in ways that employers, who'd much prefer younger, more pliable workers, might not have liked at first. This is the future that champions of globalization like Bill Clinton promised in the 1990s, when he campaigned on "building a bridge to the twenty-first century." Yes, globalization might mean that some of yesterday's jobs go away. The hope was that as Americans upgraded their skills, old jobs would quickly be replaced by newer ones that offered higher wages, and not just for the privileged few. That is not quite how things turned out. To the contrary, U.S. labor market dynamism, the process through which old jobs in declining firms are replaced by new jobs in fast-growing start-ups, has fallen sharply. This decline in dynamism has a lot to do with why globalization has become such a dirty word in American politics.

Why didn't we see an upgrading of America's jobs that extended to all workers? Part of the story is that, as I have established, the United States welcomed a large number of low-skill immigrants. Low-skill immigration ensured that low-wage employers had more than enough capable workers to choose from, and older veterans of manufacturing jobs were far from their most desirable option. Moreover, stringent local land-use regulations saw to it that the richest, most productive regions with the best labor market prospects effectively priced out domestic migrants from the Rust Belt.

Why haven't working-class natives moved en masse from struggling towns in the heartland to Palo Alto or Manhattan? Part of the story is that the money that would buy you a decent standard of living in your hometown won't go nearly as far in America's richest regions. It is not exactly that domestic migrants are priced out of the country's most productive cities; it is just that they are unable to maintain square footage and other amenities there, in either home ownership or the rental market. These are are lower priorities for low-skill immigrants, for a variety of reasons.

And if you depend on Medicaid or any other public assistance programs, you will likely have a difficult time reestablishing your eligibility in your new home.[28] The story is different for a working-class immigrant from the developing world, for whom living in overcrowded conditions on the outskirts of Queens or making an hours-long commute might still be vastly preferable to life back in the old country. If you're a recent immigrant who has just settled in the Rust Belt, there isn't that much to keep you there, especially if you're not yet eligible for most forms of public assistance. That's one reason low-skill immigrants are so much more geographically mobile in the wake of a recession than low-skill natives.[29]

At the very moment that large swaths of America's

existing working class was reckoning with the downsides of offshoring, the United States welcomed an entirely new immigrant working class, which was more geographically flexible and more desperate to get on the bottom rungs of the service economy. We didn't welcome quite enough immigrants to compete with low-wage labor in China, mind you. But we did invite enough to greatly expand the potential supply of service workers, and to prop up old low-wage business models in the service sector and create entirely new ones.

And, as I have alluded to before, low-skill immigration increases the number of people who are most vulnerable to displacement. No one knows exactly where technology will take us in the years to come. What we can say with some confidence is that the jobs and skills that are least vulnerable to automation are those that require a fair bit of education and strong communication skills. Physically demanding jobs that involve lots of routine tasks—the kind of dirty, dangerous, and difficult jobs that are disproportionately done by low-skill immigrants today—are especially vulnerable to automation. If immigration is going to keep automation at bay, it must be continuous, because if the flow of new less-skilled workers ever stops or slows, labor-saving technology will always be waiting in the wings, ready to displace workers who are doing jobs that machines can do just as well.

This is not to say that high low-skill immigration levels

couldn't keep automation at bay for a very long time. Rest assured, if we established guest-worker programs that added tens of millions of workers to the labor market, U.S. employers would find something for them to do, especially if they were exempt from the minimum wage, as Weyl and Posner have explicitly suggested. But as other countries see their low-skill populations dwindle, they will be the ones pioneering laborsaving technologies that will, over time, become cost-competitive with low-wage labor. Our continued reliance on labor-intensive business models will stand out from the rest of the developed world.

Of course, all of this assumes that there won't be a populist backlash to the prevalence of low-wage jobs in the meantime. If that does indeed happen, we can expect a move to hike minimum wages and strengthen worker protections, which in turn would raise the cost of employing low-skill workers. Automation would grow far more attractive, even if the result were higher unemployment and underemployment for low-skill workers, as we have seen in Sweden and elsewhere. The end result could be a class war like we have never seen.

Fortunately, there are other ways to better the lives of the hundreds of millions of potential migrants around the world than to welcome them en masse in the style of Qatar or Singapore. That is the subject of our next chapter.

CHAPTER FIVE

It's a Small World

Over the past few years, I've thought long and hard about the argument that the United States has a moral obligation to open its borders. As much as I reject this conclusion, I see its force. According to this line of thinking, the only relevant question in immigration policy is whether the people who now enjoy the fruits of participation in our prosperous society are any more morally worthy than the vast number of potential migrants we turn away. If they are not, there can be no justification for mass *exclusion*—the flipside of mass immigration. Given the vast number of people who'd settle in the United States if they could, and the self-reinforcing dynamics of immigration, in which the presence of a few pioneering immigrants in a city or region tends to attract their relatives, friends, and neighbors from back home, a more laissez-faire immigration system could easily mean immigration levels several times as high as what we've seen in recent years. And if that leads to more domestic inequality, or the rise of ethnic enclaves with populations in the millions? So be it.

Yet even at current levels, low-skill immigration is exacerbating many of America's challenges, as I've argued throughout the preceding chapters. Doubling or tripling low-skill immigration, or going further still, would require a truly drastic restructuring of our social order, which would create problems all its own. What I can't deny, though, is that the champions of opening America's borders have a serious point in their favor, which is that low-skill immigration really is a tremendous boon to low-skill immigrants, even when their rights and liberties are severely restricted and they're relegated to a powerless underclass, as in Qatar and other Gulf states.

Where does that leave those of us who want America to be a country that is decent and generous, not just powerful and rich? As I see it, we need to strike a new bargain. If we are going to adopt a more selective, skills-based immigration system, as I believe we should, we should also redouble our commitment to bettering the lives of people around the world, hundreds of millions of whom would happily settle

in our country if they had the chance. In the pages that follow, I sketch out a few possibilities for how the United
States might help create economic opportunities for the
billions who aren't fortunate enough to be the citizens of a
rich market democracy, yet who are no less deserving of a
chance to flourish. Some of the ideas that follow might
strike you as overly ambitious, or even fanciful. I expect
than in a few years' time, however, many of them will instead seem like common sense.

Americas First

Leaving your home country behind can be a harrowing experience. And though low-skill immigrant workers almost
always earn far more in the United States than they could in
their native countries, the cost of living in an affluent country and the difficulty of climbing from the bottom to the
middle can be demoralizing in the extreme. If migration is
your only option for a better life, you may well take it, even
if it means being far from loved ones and toiling in jobs
where poverty-level wages and a docile manner are your
only protection against being replaced by a machine. But
that doesn't make the choice to leave home any less tragic.

Ideally, we could reduce migration pressures by raising
incomes in source countries. It is an idea that's been end-
lessly pursued by politicians in rich countries hoping to

stem the tide of migration, but with little success. Michael Clemens, a champion of low-skill immigration, has found[1] that development reduces emigration only at fairly high levels of income per capita. Once a country's income per capita is in the neighborhood of $8,000 or so,[2] adjusted for purchasing power, which we can think of as the threshold for upper-middle-income status, its residents become less inclined to leave the country as their incomes rise. Before the upper-middle-income threshold is reached, however, rising income tends to spur *more* emigration, presumably because it gives truly impoverished people the means to pack up and leave. And it's not as though emigration suddenly comes to an end above the $8,000 threshold, which is, of course, a moving target; even as countries reach upper-middle-income status, emigration typically remains above the levels seen in the poorest countries, those with incomes per capita of $1,000 or below.

By way of comparison, income per capita in the United States is $59,500, and in India and Nigeria, two of the world's most populous countries, it is $7,200 and $5,900, respectively. In other words, India and Nigeria have yet to reach upper-middle-income status, and they're markedly better off than the world's poorest countries, such as Burundi and the Central African Republic. What this means is that global migration pressures are almost certain to rise as poor countries, and particularly poor countries in sub-Saharan Africa, develop. Before turning to the global scene, though, let's start by considering migration pressures in our own neighborhood, the northern half of the Americas.

Consider Mexico and Central America, which have long sent large numbers of workers to the United States. Right now, Guatemala ($8,200), Honduras ($5,500), and El Salvador ($8,900) are right at the point when you'd expect migration pressures to start easing up. They are wealthy enough that Central Americans might see rising prosperity at home as a realistic possibility. One of the reasons migration from Mexico to the United States has slowed so sharply in recent years is that Mexico's GDP per capita (PPP) is now $19,500. This is still substantially lower than income per capita in the United States, and this gap remains big enough to tempt Mexican workers northward. Yet as the standard of living has improved in Mexico, its people are less eager to leave their families and neighborhoods behind. Something similar can happen in Central America, provided the United States and Mexico work together.

Mexico has now become prosperous enough, and its population is aging quickly enough,[3] that it ought to consider welcoming more immigrants from Central America itself. The beauty of Mexico as a destination for Central American workers is that its cultural familiarity and geographical proximity, coupled with the more modest gap in living standards between Mexico and its Central American neighbors, will help ensure that migrants retain strong ties to their native countries.

Is it fair for the United States to expect Mexico to welcome more Central American migrants? Now that it has joined the ranks of upper-middle-income countries, it is not unreasonable to expect that Mexico will act as an equal partner with the United States in lifting up its neighbors. The United States already devotes considerable resources to fighting organized crime in Mexico and Central America,[4] most of which is connected to the trafficking of drugs and the smuggling of human beings. A far better use of these funds would be helping Central Americans fleeing desperate or dangerous circumstances to find refuge in Mexico and, over the long term, financing the investments that will raise the region's productive potential. And there is a great deal more the United States could do to facilitate development in neighboring countries.

One challenge is that while Mexico's per capita income places it in roughly the same ballpark as moderately well-off countries—such as Russia, Malaysia, and Turkey—Mexico, like the United States, is a highly unequal country. Until life improves for the poorest Mexicans, migration will remain an attractive option.

While Americans often rail against unauthorized immigration from Mexico, the real culprit is that the Mexican government has historically failed to provide for its own people. Unauthorized immigrants are at fault for violating

U.S. immigration laws, but their home governments, which have failed to create safe and prosperous environments in which they can raise their children, are also to blame.[5] To lose sight of that would be callous. The good news is that Mexico has made strides in reducing extreme poverty, thanks in part to the increased social spending that accompanied Mexico's political democratization. Two major anti-poverty programs in particular, Progresa and Opportunidades, have greatly increased household incomes among Mexico's poorest families. But social spending is not enough. Further reductions in poverty will depend on job creation for Mexicans with modest skills. One of the ironies of Donald Trump's embrace of protectionism is that if our goal is to reduce migration from Mexico, we ought to welcome the offshoring of industries that depend heavily on low-skill immigrant labor. Why fight to keep low-wage jobs in meatpacking, general assembly, and furniture manufacturing in the United States if these jobs tend to be held by low-skill immigrants, most of whom would much rather earn a decent living at home?

More ambitiously, the United States ought to make it easier for U.S. retirees to settle in Mexico. As the U.S. population ages, demand for home health aides and other low-wage service workers who can provide for the elderly is increasing, and this rising demand is often cited by advocates of higher immigration levels. But instead of admitting more low-skill immigrants, the United States could allow

U.S. retirees to make use of Medicare in Mexico, a simple measure that would address a number of problems at once: it would generate employment opportunities for low-skill workers in Mexico; it would reduce the demand for new low-skill immigrant workers in the United States; and it might even reduce Medicare expenditures, since the cost of offering benefits would be substantially lower in Mexico than in the United States.

If this seems unrealistic, keep in mind that a growing number of U.S. retirees were either born in or have family ties to Latin America, and many would welcome the prospect of reconnecting with their roots. Furthermore, a large population of older Americans already resides in regions like Jalisco, Guanajuato, Baja California Sur, and the Mexican Caribbean. More older Americans would join them in seeking a lower cost of living in Mexico if their Medicare benefits traveled with them. If this initiative proved successful, it could be extended to other countries in Central America and the Caribbean, and perhaps further afield. Already, a number of countries in the region, such as Panama and Belize, grant visas to retirees who can demonstrate they have enough monthly income to support themselves. In a spirit of reciprocity, the United States might welcome retirees who, similarly, pass a minimum income threshold pegged to our higher cost of living, provided they also purchase comprehensive medical insurance.

To some, encouraging U.S. retirees to live abroad will

sound positively sinister. Nothing could be further from the truth. The idea is not to force people to leave their homes behind. Rather, it is to level the playing field between moving to a retirement community in Florida and moving to a retirement community farther south, still within easy reach of loved ones back home. The proposal I've outlined will surely be met with resistance from domestic medical providers and nursing homes, who will resent the prospect of facing competition from elsewhere in the Americas. But to provide for the long-term care needs of an aging population, we will have to get creative. To get a sense of the challenge ahead, consider that as of 2017, it is estimated that there are 5.4 million Americans suffering from Alzheimer's disease, a number that is set to triple by 2050.[6] And unpaid caregivers are estimated to spend an average of almost twenty-two hours a week attending to Alzheimer's patients.[7] Given the rising proportion of older Americans who are "kinless," i.e., who have no living relatives,[8] we're looking at a massive social challenge. Right now, the plan seems to be that we will shift from unpaid caregiving by families toward professional caregiving in nursing home facilities, which will mean employing a large number of health aides and the like. Even if we were to pay these workers no more than the U.S. minimum wage—not a wage that would ensure a decent standard of living for U.S.–based caregivers and their families—the cost to families and taxpayers would be staggering. Offshoring caregiving would greatly improve the well-being of U.S. seniors and of workers in neighboring countries, most of whom would welcome an alternative to emigration.

At the same time, border hawks need to recognize that cooperation is a better way to achieve their goals than confrontation. The fates of the United States, Mexico, and the Central American states are intertwined, and securing Mexico's cooperation in curbing unauthorized immigration will likely require giving the Mexican government something it wants. Keep in mind that Mexico is not just a source of migrants to the United States—it also separates us from Guatemala, Honduras, and El Salvador, all of which are much poorer than Mexico, and where migration pressures are still building. These countries are the biggest new sources of unauthorized migration to the United States, and to control the pace of migration from Central America, we must convince the Mexican government to stop turning a blind eye when Central Americans pass through its territory en route to the United States.

The Mexican government, for all its weaknesses, is fully capable of halting Central American migrants. In 2001, for example, President Vicente Fox deployed the armed forces to prevent migrants from passing through the Sonoran Desert, out of fear that they might die of thirst in a severe heat wave.[9] Since 2014, the Mexican government has stepped up its efforts to regulate the flow of migration to the United States.[10] Instead of focusing solely on securing America's southern border, we would do well to secure Mexico's co-operation in halting migrants long before they reach it. Winning over the Mexican government by helping it create employment opportunities at home would be far wiser than trying to bully Mexico into doing our bidding, as some Americans would prefer. Just as important, it would be far more humane and constructive, and it would pave the way for a more cooperative relationship in the decades to come. In time, a deeper U.S. partnership with Mexico could serve as a model for other countries—a far cry from the acrimonious relationship we have at present.

The Magic of Megacities

The truth, though, is that while migration pressures from Mexico and Central America command much of our attention, the real action in the coming decades will be in sub-Saharan Africa and South Asia. According to UN projections, even as populations in much of the world stabilize, sub-Saharan Africa will still enjoy relatively high fertility. And so, as the economists Gordon Hanson and Craig McIntosh have observed,[11] the number of working-age adults born in the region will go from roughly half a billion to more than 1.3 billion between 2010 and 2050. That booming young population could be channeled into productive work at home, or, failing that, could seek it elsewhere. If current patterns remain the same, "the number of African-born first-generation migrants aged 15 to 64 outside of sub-Saharan Africa," Hanson and McIntosh predict, will "grow from 4.6 million to 13.4 million between 2010 and 2050," and will mostly head to relatively low-fertility Europe.[12] And even those figures, as Hanson and McIntosh acknowledge, leave out the possibility of civil wars, climate change–induced disasters, and other such push factors.

Sub-Saharan Africa is hardly the only region with a lot of poor people. According to a recent report from the World Bank, as of 2013, about 767 million people around the world were living below the international poverty line, 378 million of whom were outside of sub-Saharan Africa.[13] The percentage of the global population made up by people living in extreme poverty is on the decline, but progress is uneven across the world, and populations are still growing. Moreover, it is worth remembering that the international poverty line is fundamentally arbitrary. It grossly underestimates the number of people around the world who are desperate to better their lot. Our real long-term objective should be to help all countries achieve broad-based prosperity.

By 2050, the United Nations projects that Earth will be home to 9.8 billion people. Half of the growth between now and then will come from nine countries alone: in order, India, Nigeria, the Democratic Republic of the Congo, Pakistan, Ethiopia, Tanzania, the United States, Uganda, and

Indonesia.[14] Most of these countries are poor, and many of them are rapidly urbanizing. India's population, for example, has dramatically shifted over the past several decades. According to the Indian census, urbanization increased from about 28 percent of the population in 2001 to about 31 percent in 2011.[15] In real terms, that entailed the movement of millions of people to cities that were ill-equipped to handle them. And so, with urbanization has come an increase in inequality in India's urban areas,[16] ever growing slums (that are already home to about 26 percent of urban dwellers),[17] and a rise in urban crime rates.[18] For now, there is no end in sight. India remains home to the world's largest rural population: 857 million. By 2050, that population is expected to decline drastically as the country's urban citizenry grows by 404 million.[19] The extra pressure building up in Indian cities—and cities like them around the world—will have to go somewhere.

In short, around the world there are hundreds of millions of people looking for a better life, and there is no prospect of the United States absorbing them. Indeed, as Hanson, McIntosh, and Chen Liu argued in a 2017 paper,[20] whereas the United States saw a large influx of low-skill immigrants from Latin America from the 1970s to the 2000s, most of whom traveled overland, any wave of unauthorized immigrants from Africa and South Asia is likely to crest on European shores. Just as Europe's democracies did not volunteer to admit large numbers of low-skill immigrants from Latin America to address the demographic pressures of the previous era, it is unlikely that the United States will drastically increase its openness to low-skill immigration today rather than let Europe bear the brunt of the coming wave.

There is another complicating factor, which is the fact that East Asia might very well emerge as a magnet for migrants from Africa and South Asia. Homi Kharas of the Brookings Institution projects that by 2030, Asia will be home to 3.5 billion middle-income consumers, defined as those with incomes between $11 and $110 dollars a day, adjusted for purchasing power.[21] While some Asian countries with large rising middle classes have populations that are young and growing quickly, such as India, others, such as China, have populations that are old and growing slowly, to the point where their age structures will closely resemble that of elderly Japan. Given this landscape, it is easy to see why Africans and South Asians might be eager to make their fortunes in these countries. Yet compared to the market democracies of North America and Europe, wealthy countries in East Asia have traditionally been quite closed to immigration.

It is certainly possible that increasingly affluent East Asians will soon be convinced of the wisdom of opening their borders to low-skill immigration from countries with dramatically different cultures. Singapore, as we've discussed, has long welcomed large numbers of low-skill guest workers, so perhaps China will follow its lead. But Beijing and Seoul and other governments in the region would prefer not to import low-wage labor from abroad and will instead be eager to find other ways to better the lives of potential migrants.

Here we turn to a solution that ought to appeal to the great many Americans who admire the pioneering spirit of their forebears: We ought to promote the creation of entirely new cities, which can offer a much higher quality of governance than is now found in much of Africa and South Asia.

As fanciful as this may sound, we really have no choice. The urban population of the developing world is expected to grow from 2.6 billion to 7.8 billion over the next hundred years.[22] Much of this growth will be met by the expansion and densification of existing cities. Yet there is no question that entirely new cities will arise, as they have in earlier eras. Growing an existing city has its advantages, and many of the world's most ambitious new cities have been failures, especially when they've been built to glorify a country's rulers rather than to exploit new economic opportunities. There is, however, one very big advantage to building new cities: their founders can learn from past experiences and adopt new institutions and technologies with relatively little blowback from incumbent interests.

For years, the economist Paul Romer has championed

the idea of "charter cities," that is, new cities that are established with rules and institutions carefully designed to foster economic growth and upward mobility for the world's poor.[23] As an example, he points to the experience of Shenzhen, a teeming metropolis of more than ten million that as recently as 1980 was little more than a fishing village. To capture some of the dynamism of neighboring Hong Kong, the Chinese government established a special economic zone (SEZ) in Shenzhen that, over time, became a hub of labor-intensive manufacturing, and that has since evolved into a font of entrepreneurial growth. Of course, not all of China's SEZs were so wildly successful, and one can't expect SEZs created elsewhere to match Shenzhen. Nevertheless, Shenzhen offers an inspiring example, and capturing even a fraction of its success could do a great deal to boost incomes.

Though the notion of charter cities has been criticized as utopian, or even as "neo-colonial," it is a far more realistic solution than expecting the United States and the market democracies of Europe and East Asia to voluntarily reinvent themselves as super-sized Qatars. Cameron Abadi, writing in *Foreign Policy*,[24] has drawn attention to the work of Gerald Knaus of the European Stability Initiative, who has touted what he calls the "Rome Plan." The goal of the plan would be to secure the cooperation of migrant-sending countries in Africa by granting them a predetermined number of residence and work permits in exchange for help with immigration enforcement. So far, so appealing. But what would be the number? Judging by the mood of the European public, one has to assume it would have to be quite small—at most, we could expect flows in the hundreds of thousands, which would be met with stiff resistance. Charter cities, in contrast, could one day offer a better life to a far larger number of people.

It is already the case that a rising proportion of international migration is "south-south," or movement between relatively poor countries.[25] And this kind of migration can be enormously beneficial, as it can create a critical mass of talent where it might not otherwise exist. Right now, though, most of this migration is unauthorized, and the migrants themselves typically work in the informal sector, which makes it hard for them to climb the economic ladder. Still, that hasn't stopped people from migrating. According to *The Economist*, the Indian government estimates that as many as twenty million Bangladeshi nationals are living on Indian soil, and independent observers peg the number at fifteen million.[26] In recent years, the Bangladeshi influx has sparked intense political resistance, partly because of the fear that Bangladeshi Muslims will change India's ethnoreligious mix. And there are countless other examples of similarly fraught conflicts, particularly in Africa. Charter cities could offer an invaluable alternative.

So how might charter cities emerge? For one, necessity is sure to play a role. In 2015, the Syrian migrant crisis led

Alexander Betts and Paul Collier to devise an unorthodox solution. In a *Foreign Affairs* article,[27] they offered a plan that would resettle Syrian refugees close to home.[28] While hundreds of thousands of Syrians sought refuge in Europe, millions instead made their way to Lebanon, Jordan, and Turkey. Some have found themselves in refugee camps; others have settled in cities, where they work illegally and lead a marginal existence. Betts and Collier devised a more sustainable solution: Instead of herding refugees into camps where they are forced to subsist on aid, they called for the creation of special economic zones. Essentially, a consortium of countries, including all of the major western economies, would create financial incentives and trade concessions to spur industrial development in these zones, which would employ refugees and, in some number, citizens of the host country. With the help of the international community, these zones could become a hub for labor-intensive manufacturing and other kinds of productive economic activity. Ultimately, skills learned and firms established in these new special economic zones could be brought back to Syria once peace is reestablished there.

The beauty of Betts and Collier's approach is that it promised Syrians a measure of economic self-sufficiency and cultural autonomy in exile, and it sidestepped the challenges of integration by giving them their own space in which to flourish. Getting the Jordanians to agree to such a scheme may well be challenging. And making such industrial zones viable would require major investments not just from the host countries but also from the European Union, the United States, and rich democracies around the world, which would need to use aid dollars to convince the Jordanians to go along. Yet the costs of getting such a scheme off the ground would be a small fraction of the costs of successfully integrating refugee families into European countries that are at best ambivalent about welcoming them into their societies and economies. Ultimately, the Jordanian government agreed to experiment with special economic zones,[29] seeing them as a way to capitalize on its role as a safe haven and to contain some of the extraordinary social pressures involved in absorbing refugee migrants. Though it's too early to say the experiment has been a success, it holds great promise. To really take off, though, these special economic zones will need capital, expertise, and market access from the United States and other rich countries. We would be foolish not to provide it.

Still, these special economic zones wouldn't be charter cities as Romer envisioned them. Getting there will take time and confidence on the part of host countries that their sovereignty won't be unduly compromised and that their own citizens will benefit. It's time for Americans to roll up their sleeves and help. Eventually, charter cities could achieve the same size and scale of a city like Shenzhen, which has grown from a population of 30,000 in 1980 to more than ten million today. If English settlers could lay the foundations for great cities with new, more responsive systems of government centuries ago, why wouldn't we expect that today's migrants could do much the same if given the chance?

The Virtue of Virtual Immigration

Even if we assume that charter cities take off, and that many older Americans prove willing to retire abroad, there will still be demand for low-cost services in the United States. Thankfully, it is increasingly possible for workers in poor countries to serve customers in rich countries without ever leaving home. I've already discussed the role of offshoring in the global economy. Whether we like it or not, the next step in the offshoring revolution is likely to be virtual immigration, or what the economist Richard Baldwin has dubbed "remote intelligence."[30] Think of a meeting in which you're sitting next to a strikingly realistic holographic projection of your colleague, who lives in the South Pacific, or remote-controlled drones piloted by workers in some other faraway foreign locale that will replace today's security guards and janitors.

Many U.S. employers already rely on workers who telecommute from abroad. Because the United States is a high-productivity, high-wage society by global standards, even low-skill work commands a hefty "place premium,"[31] that is, you will earn more in the United States than in Bolivia, even if you're doing the same job—a fact that is often used to make the case for low-skill immigration. But technology also allows U.S. employers to take advantage of a "place discount," which is to say that workers in low-productivity, low-wage societies are often willing to do the same jobs for less. Living in Belarus or Indonesia can be a lot cheaper than living in Silicon Valley, which means workers can enjoy a high standard of living even while accepting a lower wage. Indeed, this has tempted many so-called "global nomads" to settle in cheap, pleasant corners of the developing world. Now imagine if high-cost services in the United States, like higher education and medical care, were disrupted by competition from skilled professionals residing in low-cost, low-wage countries. Why not hire a Filipino engineer to help you master calculus, or ask a Sudanese physician to provide you with a second opinion on a nagging health question? American consumers could reap a huge windfall.

On the other hand, virtual immigration on a mass scale would mean that service workers in America would face competition not unlike that seen by manufacturing workers in recent decades, which could cause a great deal of disruption. At the same time, there would be a very big difference between virtual immigration and real immigration, especially insofar as we as a society prefer to take an egalitarian approach, in which we welcome immigrants on a permanent basis and take meeting their basic human needs seriously, as opposed to the Qatar-style approach, in which low-skill immigrants are expected to fend for themselves. Virtual immigration offers a different bargain to those looking to better their lives: you can come work, and your wages will rise, but your material needs will continue to be met in your homeland.

The natural tendency of voters in rich market democracies will be to oppose virtual immigration, on the grounds that it will be a threat to the wages and jobs of citizens. We ought to resist that tendency, for the same reason we ought to resist barriers to trade in goods and services: there is good reason to believe that, on balance, virtual immigration will do more good than harm for U.S. workers, provided we have the right safeguards in place. And to be blunt, in light of how virtual presence technologies are advancing, I'm not sure we have the option of shutting virtual immigration down, even if we wanted to do so. Instead, we should do everything we can to make a virtue of necessity.

A Better World

In the decades to come, billions of people around the world will do everything in their power to climb out of poverty. Realistically, only a small fraction of them will be in a position to settle in the world's rich countries—this is especially true of America, which is separated from Asia and Africa by the Pacific and Atlantic Oceans. We need to do more than pat ourselves on the back for welcoming workers who have the wherewithal to travel enormous distances to better their lot. Ultimately, we must spread the know-how and the institutions that make robust economic growth possible to ensure that there are dozens of Shenzhens on every continent, within reach of all those seeking opportunity.

Obviously, the ideas I've presented for how Americans can help people around the world without embracing low-skill immigration won't satisfy everyone. So I'd like to close this chapter with two contrasting thoughts. The first might appeal to those who believe that a world in which Americans are much richer than people in the developing world is presumptively unjust, and who oppose border restrictions on those grounds. The second is for people like me, who believe that it is possible to favor low levels of low-skill immigration while also wanting to better the lives of the global poor.

While there has been much discussion of how low-skill immigration to the United States betters the lives of migrants, it is important not to neglect the fact that most people in the world's poorer countries aren't especially eager to leave home, and not all are capable of doing so, for a variety of reasons ranging from poverty to infirmity. It is worth considering the possibility that instead of calling upon the United States and other affluent democracies to welcome more low-skill immigrants, global egalitarians in these countries should consider moving to countries in the developing world where low-skill labor is abundant. One of the chief economic arguments for low-skill immigration is that it can complement high-skill workers in developed countries, as we have seen. Yet the logic also holds true in reverse: when high-skill workers move to the developing world, they can often make great gains in their standard of living, particularly if they are eager to employ domestic help. Assuming they continue to earn high incomes, the resulting tax revenues can then help finance social services for people who are often drastically poorer than even the poorest Americans.[32]

In 1957, J. B. S. Haldane, a celebrated British scientist, decided to leave his native country to settle in India, where he became a naturalized citizen shortly before his death.[33] Haldane was famously idealistic, and he concluded that moving to India would best suit his socialist and humanist convictions. I don't imagine I'd have agreed with Haldane on very much. He was, among other things, an admirer of the Soviet Union, something he had in common with many of the leading lights of India's ruling Congress Party at the time. What I will say, though, is that when it came to his egalitarian beliefs, Haldane was willing to put his money where his mouth was: he didn't just pay lip service to his cosmopolitan ideals; he moved to a country where he believed he could do the most good.

There's another approach, though, which I associate

with the renowned agricultural scientist Norman Borlaug, the Nobel laureate who famously sparked the Green Revolution, which greatly increased agricultural yields throughout the developing world.[34] I can't speak to Borlaug's views on immigration—as he was the son of Norwegian immigrants, I wouldn't be at all surprised if he was favorably disposed to it. But while Haldane lived up to his ideals by moving to India, Borlaug lived up to his own by creating tools that allowed millions of poor farmers in the developing world to not only survive but to flourish, a development that later paved the way for prosperity-boosting urbanization and industrialization.

There will always be a place for the Haldanes of the world with their utopian visions of the future. Yet there is an equally important place for the Borlaugs, who offer practical solutions for the here and now. We need them both.

CHAPTER SIX

Nation Building

Picture the United States in the year 2036, in a world in which the melting pot ideal has made a triumphant return. After the political turmoil and social unrest of the late 2010s and early 2020s, it seemed as though America's divides might never heal. In the bad old days, the color of one's skin had seemed to determine one's fate. Faith in the American experiment had diminished as demagogues on the right and left whipped up fear and resentment. Sensing a profound danger to civil peace, a handful of visionary leaders crafted a new grand bargain in 2024, adopting a more moderate and restrained immigration policy while increasing investment in the potential of children of all colors and class backgrounds.

Twelve years later, America is hardly a utopia, but the bargain is working. Productivity growth has reached unprecedented heights, which in turn has translated into robust wage and income growth for all American workers. Ethnic distinctions that once seemed to be of existential importance have faded into insignificance. Americans still find plenty to fight about, but the country's melting-pot culture, newly enriched by influences from Latin America, Asia, and Africa, has proven a unifying force.

Though America's population of 370 million is dwarfed by those of India and China, the country remains uniquely powerful on the world stage, thanks in part to its decision to form stronger economic and strategic partnerships with its neighbors in the Americas, most of which now have booming economies. At the same time, American capital and know-how has helped get dozens of new charter cities off the ground in Africa and South Asia. These magnets for migrants have become fonts of entrepreneurship and public policy solutions, and it is now common for ideas developed in these new Shenzhens to make their way to America's vibrant metropolises. And in these metropolises, young people of color no longer feel like second-class citizens who must fight tooth and nail for dignity and respect. In the America of 2036, stability and opportunity are a concrete fact-of-life for all citizens, not just for a privileged few.

Getting to this America will require recognition that the reason immigration must be reformed is not increased crime or downward wage pressure. Immigration must be reformed because in its current character, it is undermining civic solidarity, producing ethnic balkanization, and breeding polarized backlash. In this chapter, I want to offer a new approach to immigration and integration, which will engender American solidarity. Some of my ideas have long been championed by immigration restrictionists, including Donald Trump; others will be harder for many of my allies on the right to accept. Yet I'm convinced that my three proposals—offering amnesty to the long-resident unauthorized population, adopting a skills-based immigration system, and fighting the intergenerational transmission of poverty—will, taken together, help make America a middle-class melting pot.

The Amnesty Wars

Think back to the summer of 2016, when Democrats and Republicans pitted Dreamers against Angel Moms. At the 2016 Democratic National Convention in late July, one of the more noteworthy speakers was Astrid Silva, a twenty-eight-year-old progressive activist from Nevada. Silva was one of the Dreamers, a catchall term dreamed up by immigration activists for the roughly 1.8 million unauthorized youth who were brought into the country as minors. To her,

Donald Trump's calls for deporting unauthorized migrants weren't an abstraction. They were a direct threat to the life she and her family had built in America since she was a toddler. Silva's deeply personal address made Trump's calls for mass deportations more vivid, and more harrowing. She called out the Republican presidential nominee for wanting to tear families like hers apart, and she did so to rousing applause from the assembled delegates.

It's easy to see why immigration activists wanted to make the immigration debate all about Dreamers like Silva, a hard-working, well-spoken young woman who is so clearly culturally American. By doing so, they took the immigration debate out of the realm of abstraction—what is the immigration policy that will best serve Americans as a whole?—and zeroed in on the sympathetic stories of individuals. They allowed us to forget, for a moment at least, that any limit on immigration will disadvantage tens of millions of good-hearted, decent people all around the world, all of whom no doubt have moving personal stories of their own.

Normally, it has been the advocates of increased immigration levels who were best at crafting stories that tugged at voters' heartstrings: telling stories of beloved parents and grandparents and great-grandparents who moved to America from elsewhere, pointing to the miserable poverty that plagues other nations while carefully avoiding any discussion of what it would mean to completely open America's borders to the global poor. These narratives were, by the summer of 2016, already very familiar, but then something strange happened. Restrictionists pushed back with harrowing stories of their own.

Just over a month after Silva's DNC address, at a rally in Phoenix, Arizona, Donald Trump called a very different set of witnesses to make their case on the national stage: "Angel Moms," a group of women who had lost a family member in the course of a violent crime committed by an unauthorized immigrant. One by one, the mothers recounted their painful stories of loss. Maureen Maloney's twenty-three-year-old son Matthew "was dragged a quarter mile to his death by an illegal alien"; Mary Ann Mendoza's son Brandon, a thirty-two-year-old police officer, was killed "in a violent head-on collision" with an unauthorized immigrant driving drunk who had previously been convicted of crimes but never deported. The women thanked Trump profusely and asserted that if he had been president, the border would have been secure and their family members' lives might have been saved.

To many Republicans, Silva's address at the DNC was a cynical maneuver, an effort to put a hopeful and optimistic face on uncontrolled immigration and mislead the public about its destructive effects on American society. To many Democrats, meanwhile, the Angel Moms' presentation amounted to a vicious and unfounded slander against immigrants, a stunt every bit as bigoted as if Trump had paraded the families of victims of crimes committed by African

Americans. Regardless of whom you sympathize with, these two competing acts of political theater illustrate the way the clashing sides in our increasingly vituperative immigration debate have become unrecognizable to each other.

Advocates of a large-scale amnesty often observe, correctly, that a majority of Americans are open to the idea of legalizing a large number of unauthorized immigrants. And, according to the Pew Research Center, an overwhelming 74 percent majority support granting legal status to the Dreamers.[1] Inevitably, granting legal status to the Dreamers raises the question of what we ought to do for the parents of the Dreamers, many of whom also live in the United States as unauthorized immigrants. Indeed, many amnesty opponents see the emphasis on the Dreamers as a salami-slicing tactic— an effort to use the most sympathetic unauthorized immigrants to divide the opposition and to make the case for the most expansive amnesty possible. Many also rightly resent the suggestion that their opposition to amnesty stems from racism. As the political scientists Morris Levy and Matthew Wright, both of whom are sympathetic to legalization for unauthorized immigrants, have found, however, much of the opposition is, in fact, driven by a commitment to the rule of law.[2] That is, while amnesty advocates tend to see the issue in attribute-based terms—they want to grant unauthorized immigrants legal status on the basis of their individual characteristics, such as their work ethic and their overall ability to make a positive contribution to the country—amnesty opponents are more inclined to make categorical judgments, in which individual merits aren't really the issue: you could be a truly terrific person, but you still broke the law and you shouldn't be rewarded for having done so. The law is the law. Levy and Wright find that as many as one-third of Americans reject the idea of an amnesty for unauthorized immigrants on these grounds, without regard for ethnicity or class.[3] This camp isn't about to budge.

At the same time, amnesty advocates have also dug in their heels. As of 2014, roughly two-thirds of unauthorized-immigrant adults had been in the United States for ten years or more, and only 14 percent had been in the country for five years or fewer. Out of sympathy for unauthorized immigrants who've lived in the United States for many years, amnesty advocates tend to oppose credible interior enforcement measures. For example, one of the more straightforward ways to discourage unauthorized immigration would be to modernize the E-Verify program, which is designed to help employers determine whether new hires can be lawfully employed, and to make it mandatory. Yet amnesty advocates oppose mandatory E-Verify, precisely on the grounds that it would make it hard for members of the long-resident unauthorized population to find work or to change jobs.

Reconciling these two camps might seem impossible, not least because amnesty opponents are deeply skeptical

that a new large-scale amnesty would be accompanied by
resolute enforcement to ensure that there aren't calls for yet
another amnesty in the years to come.[4] And I'm sympathetic to this point of view, as it really is true that the last
large-scale amnesty—the Immigration Reform and Control
Act of 1986 (IRCA), which ultimately granted legal status
to three million unauthorized immigrants—was followed
by further surges in unauthorized immigration. Nevertheless, I believe there is a way forward.

First, we have to acknowledge that the growth of America's unauthorized immigrant population did not happen by
accident. Several years ago, the legal scholars Eric Posner
and Adam Cox observed that the United States had a de
facto "illegal immigration system," stemming from "the de-
liberate underenforcement of immigration law plus peri-
odic amnesties."[5] The idea, in essence, is that by mostly
turning a blind eye to unauthorized entries and to visa
overstays, and allowing unauthorized immigrants to work
without much in the way of interference, the United States
put out the welcome mat, and it is hardly surprising that
millions of people took their chances, especially since the
only unauthorized immigrants who were targeted for deportation seemed to be those who had committed serious
non-immigration crimes. As Boston College political scientist Peter Skerry, writing in *National Affairs* in 2013, put it,
"just as the circumstances faced by illegal immigrants in

our country are simultaneously threatening and encouraging, so the nation's attitude toward illegals has long been at once hostile and welcoming."[6] It's no wonder why amnesty advocates find the thought of mass deportation so horrifying, and why they've been so vigorously opposed to the Trump administration's efforts to deport long-resident unauthorized immigrants who've led entirely peaceful lives: it strikes them as a profoundly unfair change in the rules of the game.

Meanwhile, amnesty opponents find themselves in a tough spot. More and more, they are denounced as hateful extremists, despite the fact that most are chiefly motivated by a concern about the rule of law. Their "never never" stance on legalization has resulted in fifteen years of stalemate, which is good insofar as the goal is to preserve the immigration status quo. However, it is bad insofar as the status quo has meant that the other side continues to resist mandatory E-Verify, and state and local governments in immigrant-rich regions are growing increasingly unwilling to cooperate with federal immigration enforcement efforts, to the point where we might find ourselves with another nullification crisis.

Fortunately, there is another path: a large-scale amnesty followed by resolute enforcement. David Martin, a veteran of the Clinton and Obama administrations, has argued that whereas the IRCA amnesty really was followed by a

shambolic response, we now have much better tools to ensure that the legalization of the long-resident unauthorized
population would be followed by stable and efficient enforcement.[7] Specifically, Martin points to tools that would
allow the federal government to more effectively crack down
on visa overstayers, who represent a rising share of new
unauthorized immigrants. The key would be mandatory
E-Verify, which would become more palatable once long-
resident unauthorized immigrants are granted legal status.
This would address the most sympathetic cases.

Wouldn't such an amnesty create an incentive for new
unauthorized immigrants to try their luck, as happened after the IRCA amnesty? Not if enforcement is, indeed,
strengthened. It may well be the case that if someone who
left your hometown in El Salvador or Bangladesh fifteen
years ago was granted legal status, you'd be tempted to follow her. However, concurrent and visible returns of people
who tried to enter the United States unlawfully in the last
month or the last year would send a much stronger counter-
vailing signal. The federal government now has the tools to
make resolute enforcement possible. The real challenge is
that advocates for unauthorized immigrants are pressing the
courts to issue broad injunctions against enforcement efforts, which have been fueled in no small part by the inclusion of long-term unauthorized residents in deportation
sweeps. Like it or not, only a large-scale amnesty has any
hope of changing this dynamic.

The Point of a Points System

As I write, roughly two-thirds of the green cards issued every year are given to the family members of U.S. citizens and lawful permanent residents. For years, there's been a growing consensus among immigration reformers on the left and right that we ought to consider rebalancing the influx, to place greater emphasis on skills.[8] At the same time, however, Americans are broadly sympathetic to family-based admissions,[9] and when explicitly asked about whether we ought to cut them, much of the public objects. It's a bit like public opinion about the size of government: there are many Americans who will endorse the idea of a smaller government in the abstract, but when pressed on which government programs they'd like to see cut in practice, they'll recoil, or say they only want to cut foreign aid. So how can advocates of a more selective, skills-based system move the ball forward? First, we need to cut through some confusion.

Advocates of a more permissive immigration policy have pushed back hard against limits on family-based admissions, and they are taking a number of different tacks. For one, they've emphasized the rising educational attainment of family-based immigrants. In recent years, 47 percent of family-based immigrant adults have had college degrees, as compared to roughly one-third of U.S.–born adults. But as we'll see, this actually tells us less than you might think.

There is no question that the rate of college attainment among U.S. immigrants has risen dramatically since the mid-2000s. Between 2011 and 2015, almost half of immigrants who came to the United States were college graduates.[10] That compares to 31 percent of adults born in this country. The largest number of new immigrants with college degrees came from Asia, with India and China as the two biggest sending countries in that group. And, at 50 percent, Asia had the largest proportion of immigrants with college degrees to total adult immigrants.[11] The second-largest number of college-educated immigrants came from Latin America, although Latin America had the lowest share—13 percent—of college grads to all immigrant adults.[12] As a result of these trends, even though this period saw decreases in the flow of immigrants to the United States, between 2000 and 2015, the population of foreign-born college graduates in the United States increased by 90 percent.[13]

Why would we bother moving to a more skills-based system if our existing system is yielding so many college graduates? For one, educational attainment, or the number of years students are enrolled in school, isn't a very useful indicator on its own. A year spent at a high-quality school will yield much bigger gains in learning than a year spent at a low-quality school, as you might expect. It follows that there are big differences in literacy and numeracy skills among, for example, college graduates across countries, as the economists Eric Hanushek and Ludger Woessmann have documented.[14] There are, of course, higher-quality and lower-quality schools in every country. But average differences in school quality are one explanation for why credentials acquired in one country don't necessarily translate into marketable skills in another.

According to the Center for Immigration Studies (CIS), which favors a cut in immigration levels, 26 percent of households headed by college-educated immigrants rely on means-tested safety-net benefits as opposed to 13 percent of households headed by college-educated natives.[15] Critics have attacked the CIS for using households for comparison, as immigrants tend to have larger families. This is true. Yet it is also true that labor market outcomes for college-educated immigrants depend on more than just paper credentials.

Consider the contrast between two different college-educated immigrants: The first is an Indonesian with a computer science degree from an elite university in Singapore, who now works in Berlin. She speaks English fluently and has secured a lucrative job offer from a U.S. tech company. The second is an Indonesian with a humanities degree from a lower-quality local institution, who does not have a job offer and has only a rudimentary command of English. He does, however, have a sister who is a naturalized U.S. citizen and who is willing to sponsor him for a green card.

Both of these immigrants are positively selected, as they're both highly educated relative to the Indonesian population at large. Moreover, it is likely that both are drawn from Indonesia's upper class, which gives them class-specific resources they can use to navigate American life, as we discussed in chapter two. Still, it is a safe bet the earnings trajectory of the English-speaking immigrant with a lucrative job offer will be different from that of her counterpart.

This is the point where an admissionist might object that a more selective, skills-based system would amount to "central planning," a critique to which we'll return. But let's not forget that as currently constituted, family-based admissions are a confusing welter of preference categories and per-country limits that have all sorts of perverse outcomes.[16]

There are two broad subtypes of family-based admissions. The first is immediate relatives—spouses, unmarried minor children, and parents—of adult citizens. There are no limits on this category, which can be understood as capturing the "nuclear family." The second subtype is called "family preference immigrants," and it includes four categories, ranked in order of preference: (1) unmarried adult sons and daughters of citizens, (2a) spouses and minor children of legal permanent residents and (2b) unmarried sons and daughters of legal permanent residents, (3) married children of citizens, and (4) siblings of adult U.S. citizens. Both subtypes would benefit from reform.

Consider the "immediate relatives" category. As the Princeton sociologist Marta Tienda has observed, the aged parents of naturalized citizens represent a surprisingly large share of new lawful permanent residents every year, which in turn is "exacerbating the greying of the U.S. population."[17] A number of recent immigration proposals, including the RAISE Act proposed by Arkansas senator Tom Cotton and Georgia senator David Perdue, stipulate that rather than grant green cards without limit to the parents of U.S. citizens, we'd instead give them five-year renewable nonimmigrant visas, on the condition that sponsors can finance adequate health insurance for them. This provision would ensure that citizens can care for their parents, and it would make it somewhat harder for them to shift the costs of doing so to taxpayers at large.

And as for the family preference categories, current backlogs have proven enormously frustrating to sponsors. Why not prioritize among family preference immigrants in a more coherent way, for example, by prioritizing among them through the use of a RAISE-style points system?

To elaborate, the RAISE Act introduces a points system, which gives applicants points on the basis of their age, educational credentials, English-language fluency, salary offers from U.S. employers, and more. The goal of the points system is to identify immigrants who will at a minimum be in a position to provide for themselves and their families, which already narrows the pool of applicants dramatically, and ideally to identify those who will make the most substantial economic contributions. Applicants who pass the minimum thirty-point eligibility threshold would be invited to file full applications for green cards, and 140,000 employment-based visas would then be issued every year to the highest-scoring applicants.

But there's a simple tweak that could greatly improve family-based admissions: under RAISE, potential immigrants applying for family preference visas are either grandfathered in (if they were going to be granted green cards in the next year) or they are given points if they reapply for green cards through the points system. The idea is to only extend this benefit to those who are already on the wait-list. It would be simple, though, to keep assigning points to people who now qualify under the family preference categories. The Canadians do something similar, on the grounds that having relatives in the country increases an immigrant's "adaptability."

Because moving toward a more selective and skills-based system is so controversial, holding the number of green cards steady will likely be an important part of winning over at least some of the opposition. Phasing out the family preference categories, reallocating those visas to employment-based visas, and then adopting a points system that gives some (slight) weight to family ties strikes me as a workable compromise, provided an amnesty is part of the deal.

But what about the argument against central planning? Is it not foolish to assume that a points system will identify every single person who is capable of flourishing in the

United States? That is absolutely true. The argument is also, I would suggest, a bit of a red herring.

One useful way to think about our current system is that, as Posner and Cox have observed,[18] it uses both ex ante and ex post screening systems to evaluate whether a given petitioner ought to be granted the right to live and work in the United States on a permanent basis. Ex ante systems make use of pre-entry characteristics, such as educational attainment or language skills, while ex post systems rely on post-entry characteristics. These systems allow migrants into the country on a provisional basis and then either deport all those who aren't up to snuff (or, alternatively, not convert their temporary visas into permanent ones) or offer permanent visas to those who do make the cut.

Under the status quo, the formal U.S. immigration system relies heavily on ex ante screening. We assume that having a relative who is willing to sponsor you is a good proxy for being in a position to thrive in America, despite the fact that, as we have seen, a fairly high proportion of immigrant-headed households depends on means-tested benefits of one kind or another.[19] Adopting a points system would simply mean moving from one kind of ex ante screening to a modified version of it, which would take into account characteristics that can better predict economic self-sufficiency.

Moreover, a points system could also be seen as a way to improve the U.S. approach to ex post screening. Most new green cards are issued to people who already reside in the

United States and have sought to adjust their status.[20] This category includes a large and growing number of people who entered the United States on nonimmigrant work visas, such as the H-1B visa, through which employers can hire high-skill foreign workers. H-1B holders can adjust their status by applying for relatively scarce employment-based green cards or, in some cases, by marrying U.S. citizens, which unlocks access to family visas. In effect, a well-designed points system would create an easier path for high-skill workers who have demonstrated that they can support themselves while in the country on nonimmigrant visas. Instead of scrambling for a small number of employment-based visas, which are often issued on vexingly arbitrary grounds, they'd have the benefit of a more transparent and predictable system, albeit one that would set a high bar for them to clear.

Moving to an immigration system that places greater emphasis on the earning potential of future immigrants, and that incorporates the valuable information provided by job offers from U.S. employers, would go a long way toward ending America's immigration wars. Already, Americans are less divided on immigration than you might think. If the question is whether we ought to admit more immigrants or fewer of them, you'll certainly find disagreement. But when you ask about the kind of immigrants we should admit, there is something close to a consensus. Political scientists Jens Hainmueller and Daniel J. Hopkins have found that preferences vary relatively little according to education, partisanship, labor market position, or the respondent's level of ethnocentrism.[21] Given a choice, Americans of all types strongly favor admitting highly educated, English-speaking immigrants in high-status jobs. A RAISE-style points system would help accomplish that goal.

Many who share my concerns about our current immigration policies favor both a rebalancing of immigrant admissions toward those with higher skills and earning potential, as I outline here, and a net reduction in immigration levels. Both approaches are, in my view, defensible. I advocate rebalancing over reductions, in part on the grounds that an increase in high-skill immigration can help finance our efforts to promote integration and upward mobility for all Americans.

Investing in the Next Generation

I have argued that we have no choice but to accept the generational challenge of integrating large numbers of unauthorized immigrants. For one thing, there are millions of such immigrants who are the parents and siblings of U.S. citizens and lawful permanent residents, and most Americans don't have the stomach to remove them. But given the scale of this challenge, and the fact that the unauthorized low-skill immigrants we're inviting in from the shadows today are vulnerable to economic competition from future low-skill arrivals, we also ought to declare that enough is enough: this will be the last low-skill wave that we will absorb for some time to come, and this will also be the last amnesty.

Granting legal status to this population means, in effect, that we as a country are taking responsibility for its well-being. In other words, we allowed the unauthorized population to grow, we benefited from its labor, and now we have an obligation to provide for it. So it helps to understand how households headed by unauthorized immigrants are faring. Drawing on data from the 2011 American Community Survey and the 2008 Survey of Income and Program Participation, the Migration Policy Institute released a detailed profile of the unauthorized population in 2013,[22] and the results were eye-opening. Just under one third (32 percent) of unauthorized immigrant adults lived in families below the poverty level, and 62 percent lived in families earning less than 200 percent of the poverty level. Only 14 percent lived in families earning more than 400 percent of the federal poverty level, the cutoff for Obamacare subsidies. A narrow 51 percent majority of unauthorized children lived in families earning less than the federal poverty level, 78 percent lived in families earning less than 200 percent of the poverty level, and only 8 percent lived in families earning more than 400 percent. This is despite the fact that employment among unauthorized immigrants is high: 79 percent of men and 48 percent of women were employed in 2011.[23] This makes for a total of just under 7.25 million unauthorized laborers in the U.S. workforce, a figure that doesn't include those who do informal work.

The United States will also have to contend with an aging population of low-skill immigrants. Gordon Hanson, Chen Liu, and Craig McIntosh estimate that by 2030, the population of over-forty immigrants will increase by 8.5 million (81 percent), and so "we should expect sizeable growth in the number and fraction of individuals relying on public safety-net programs as a result of past and future immigration," the costs of which will mostly be shouldered by state and local governments, assuming current rules remain in place.[24] For now, these costs are somewhat contained by the fact that, as Hanson et al. estimate, somewhere between half and three-fifths of low-income foreign-born adults are unauthorized. An amnesty will change that.

Suffice it to say, providing for these older immigrants will be a challenge. My chief interest, though, is in the younger generation. I have touched on the fact that the child poverty rate in the United States is higher than that for most other wealthy countries. I've also established that children raised in immigrant-headed households are disproportionately likely to be poor. My greatest fear is that a decade or two from now, we will find that today's poor kids, and particularly the many millions of them with immigrant parents, will conclude that America has failed them, and that they will spend the rest of their lives on the margins of our society. Or, as their numbers grow, these disaffected Americans might lead a populist backlash against an establishment that does not serve them. Under these circumstances, our already threadbare social fabric might come undone.

And that is why we need to make a big investment in our young, and especially in those who are being raised in low-income households. Right now, the United States has a number of programs, such as the child tax credit (CTC), earned income tax credit (EITC), Temporary Assistance for Needy Families (TANF), and SNAP, that are designed to help families in need. In fact, the United States actually spends more now on families with children than it ever has.[25]

The problem is that, with the exception of TANF, which has been pared back, and food stamps, the government's main anti-poverty programs bypass the poorest of the poor. On a certain level, this makes sense. In particular, the CTC and EITC are paid out as tax refunds, which means that a recipient has to have a job and pay taxes to receive them.[26] They thus do a reasonably good job of encouraging people to work, which is a very good thing. Immigrant-headed households are particularly likely to work long hours at low wages, and so these programs do them a great deal of good. However, children whose parents do not or cannot work— that is, children who are likeliest to live in the deepest poverty—are left out. Almost 25 percent of families with children under the age of eighteen who have incomes below the poverty line receive no tax subsidies or food stamps.[27]

This is a serious problem, both for the children themselves and for the United States as a whole. There is no question that we should try to incentivize work. But we need to make sure that the children of parents who can't work aren't punished as a result. In chapter two, I delved into the fact that living in poverty has major effects on life outcomes for children, whether their parents are native- or foreign-born: the sociologists Robert Lee Wagmiller and Robert M. Adelman, for example, have found that those who spent at least one year in poverty as a child were more than ten times as likely to be poor at thirty-five.[28] Impoverished children are also less healthy and have lower academic achievement.[29] And on a societal level, these children are likely to struggle to make ends meet as they grow into adulthood, a fact that will cause untold heartache and resentment.

One way to break the cycle would be to create a universal child benefit. The logic is simple: some studies have shown that an additional $1,000 a year can reduce the probability of a baby being born with a low birthweight by at least two percent.[30] Others have found that the same increase can raise a child's test scores for math and reading.[31] A cash allowance, it seems, can enable parents to better invest in their children's development and can ease economic and psychological stress in the family.[32]

What might a new child benefit cost? One version, put forward by the economists Marianne P. Bitler, Annie Laurie Hines, and Marianne Page,[33] would involve an annual $2,000 benefit sent out in monthly installments to all families with children. The program would cost $142 billion a year, but it could mostly be financed by repurposing funding from the CTC and the child-related parts of the EITC. It would drastically increase the money handed out to the poorest families, although it would decrease the benefits that go to nearly poor families. Another model, designed by a group of researchers writing for the Russell Sage Foundation,[34] likewise proposes a monthly allowance—this time equaling $3,000 a year—but suggests that the sum could be tiered by the age of the child and the number of children in a household. A child under six, for example, could receive $300 a month ($3,600 a year) whereas an older child would get $250 ($3,000 a year). It should go without saying that these proposals would be enormously expensive, certainly in the short term. Adopting a more selective, skills-based immigration system would go a long way toward meeting the cost of such a program, as higher-income immigrants could be expected to pay higher taxes and consume fewer social services over the course of their working lives. But even if that weren't the case, when we consider the very real risk that many of today's poor kids will find themselves part of marginalized minorities as adults, I fear the alternative to investing in their well-being would prove far more costly, and far more dangerous.

Healing Our Divides

Amnesty will be a tough pill to swallow for border hawks, but if coupled with resolute enforcement, it can lay the groundwork for an immigration system that better serves the national interest. By favoring skilled immigrants with high earning potential, adopting a flexible points system would tilt immigrant admissions toward those who will have the most positive net fiscal impact. Rather than making it harder to sustain generous social programs that would serve all Americans, whether native-born or naturalized, this would make it much easier to do so. A more selective, skills-based immigration policy would disproportionately benefit low-skill workers who already reside in the United States, many of whom are immigrants themselves. And an expanded child credit would improve the life prospects of all of America's kids, including those who belong to the fast-growing second generation.

Taken in isolation, any one of these policies has its weaknesses, but as a package deal, they have the potential to break us out of our immigration impasse. Instead of sharpening our political and economic divides, as our broken immigration system has been doing for a generation, a new approach could actually help soften them. Far from being an anti-immigration agenda, the foregoing policies would put our immigration system on a sounder footing—an essential task at a time when our economy is being transformed by automation and offshoring and low-skill workers feel more vulnerable than ever.

Conclusion

When I was a kid, New York City felt like a tinderbox. In the winter of 1986, a group of white teens savagely assaulted a group of young black men, one of whom died while trying to escape the melee. For several months stretching from 1988 to 1989, black protesters boycotted a number of Korean-owned grocery stores, on the grounds that black customers had been unfairly singled out as potential shoplifters and even roughed up by shopkeepers. And in the summer of 1991, riots broke out in Crown Heights after an Orthodox Jewish man crashed his car into the home of a Guyanese immigrant family, killing the family's young son. These incidents were only the most vivid manifestations of a general sense that the city was coming undone. Throughout these years, violent crime was terrifyingly high, and Brooklyn, my native borough, was a watchword for joblessness and urban decay. In *The Bonfire of the Vanities*, one of Tom Wolfe's characters memorably described Brooklyn's remaining bourgeois enclaves as little white Hong Kongs amidst a sea of black and brown poverty. These were years when New Yorkers of all colors fled the city in droves, and those of us who remained feared that class and racial conflict might at any moment spin out of control.

Yet eventually the fever broke, and New York City made a dramatic comeback. Brooklyn's renaissance was particularly impressive. Neighborhoods that had once been scarred by crime transformed into magnets for bright young go-getters from around the country and around the world, seemingly overnight. The bad old days have faded into memory. A big part of the story is that immigrants have revitalized many neighborhoods that had been abandoned over the course of successive rounds of middle-class flight, which is one of the many reasons why I would never describe myself as anti-immigration, let alone anti-immigrant. I have seen living proof of all the good immigration can do.

At the same time, however, I have come to believe it is possible for the pace of change to be too fast, to the point where established Americans and newcomers come to see one another as irreconcilable strangers. One of the underappreciated truths about assimilation is that it is a two-way street. Over time, newcomers adopt many of the cultural practices of the established population, a process that is very familiar. Yet the lives of established Americans are also shaped by the presence of new arrivals in their neighborhoods and schools. This process of adjustment usually happens without fanfare, and it is usually led by children. Young people might find themselves steeped in one set of ideas and traditions at home, but as they make their way in the world, they can build their own little hybrid cultures, rooted in clusters of friends from different backgrounds. Distinctions that were once sharp start to soften, and people who once seemed foreign to us become less so.

Can this process of cultural fusion work again, and save us from becoming a nation of hostile strangers? This book is about creating the structural conditions we would need to avoid intensifying ethnic conflict. What I have not done, and what I would like to close on, is to make a personal appeal: If we are going to avoid turning America itself into a tinderbox, we will need a critical mass of people, young and old, who are willing to meet others halfway, even if that means risking embarrassment or alienating some of the members of your own cultural tribe. It is these boundary-crossers who have long greased the wheels of cultural fusion and change and who have always played a vital role in American life.

When I look to American politics, though, I am struck by the utter absence of boundary-crossers of this sort: people who have a foot in more than one camp, and who make an effort to ensure that channels of communication remain open and that compromises can still be reached. These voices are especially lacking when it comes to immigration, where I would argue we need them most. Favoring a more selective, skills-based immigration system does not make you a sinister xenophobe, and not every proponent of a large-scale amnesty is an open borders zealot. There are deals to be struck, provided we are willing to give one another an inch.

ACKNOWLEDGMENTS

My biggest debt in writing this book, and one of my biggest debts in life, is to my sisters, Rifat and Anjum, who first came to the United States as small children. They both had a tough time in those early years, not least because they were extremely close to our grandparents, who loved them dearly. But they put up a brave front, understanding even then that our parents needed all the help they could get. That is also why they changed my diapers as a baby and looked after me when our parents were away at work or school. More than anyone else, they taught me how to navigate life and how to think for myself. Though I am confident my sisters will disagree with much of what I have written in this book, they deserve at least some of the blame for it. From an early age, they nourished my curiosity and instilled me with confidence. They made me feel as though

I had worthwhile things to say, even when I was totally, completely, and disastrously wrong.

Bria Sandford, my infinitely patient editor, saw promise in this book when it was just the germ of an idea, and she and her team at Sentinel have guided me with thoughtfulness and generosity ever since. As an editor myself, it is my fondest hope that she will one day write for me. Short of that, I ask only that she continue listening to my harebrained ideas. My agent, Rafe Sagalyn, has been my indefatigable champion, as has the National Review Institute, which has been unstinting in its support of me in this and other endeavors. At a time when other think tanks have grown more intellectually exclusionary, Lindsay Craig has ensured that NRI remains a big and welcoming tent. The same is true of *National Review*, where I have the honor of working closely with our editor-in-chief, Rich Lowry. For almost a decade, Rich has been pressing me to make my writing "more Reihan." I hope I haven't let him down.

In 2015, the Institute of Politics at the University of Chicago kindly invited me to join them as a fellow, and that experience helped me develop and shape many of the ideas I set out here. It also led me to meet Theo Knights, an invaluable interlocutor who, in the years since, has provided me with hours of research help. So, too, has Jason Willick, one of America's finest young writers, who has been a crucial sounding board throughout this process. I only hope I can be as valuable to him when he writes his first book.

When I first started thinking about this project, immigration was already a fraught subject. In the months that followed, it only grew more so, which is why I so appreciate the friends who have helped me think through these issues, even when they take strong exception to my positions. Michael Lind has done more to inform and challenge my thinking than almost any other person. He is a brilliant iconoclast and an invaluable mentor. For a number of years, I wrote a column for *Slate*, where I worked closely with my dear friend Josh Levin. He helped me present my ideas to an audience that wasn't always entirely receptive to them, including a number of ideas that appear in this book. Graeme Wood and Sasha Polakow-Suransky, both of whom I have known since we were teenagers, pored over this manuscript with care and attention, and I would not have been able to finish this book without them. Though I haven't known Dimitri Halikias and Amalia Halikias for nearly as long, they graciously provided me with detailed comments that pushed me to rethink a number of points. Arpit Gupta and Tino Sanandaji helped broaden my perspective by sharing insights drawn from economic history and the comparative study of migration. Steve Teles has been an endless source of reading recommendations and wise advice. Thanks are also due to Ross Douthat, David Frum, Yuval Levin, and J. D. Vance, with whom I have long discussed and debated the challenges of immigration and integration. Without the help of these and other colleagues and friends, this book would have contained many more errors. But it must be said that all errors that remain are my own.

I have benefited enormously from the tireless work of immigration scholars at the Migration Policy Institute on the left, the Center for Immigration Studies on the right, and the champions of more open borders at the Center for Global Development, whom I admire for the clarity of their thinking and the passion of their advocacy. Though I am sure they will reject my conclusions, I deeply value their contributions.

One of the ironies of my life is that while my parents uprooted themselves to move half a world away to America, I now live a short subway ride away from the house in which I grew up. Their American-born son is as parochial as they are adventurous. In fairness, though, if they weren't quite so lovable, it is possible I would have long since moved elsewhere.

Most of all, I am grateful to Katie, who did me the kindness of allowing me to procrastinate further on this book by agreeing to marry me. At a moment when American politics seemed particularly rancorous, and just about everyone in the world seemed to go insane with rage, I met you, my all-time favorite person. And though my elation at having found you did distract me a bit, you have lifted me up in every respect. Sadly for you, writing this book is only the first of many occasions I will lean on your kindness, your intelligence, and your love.

NOTES

INTRODUCTION

1. Sen, Sudhi Ranjan. "ISIS Considers Indian Recruits Inferior to Arabs, Treats Them as Cannon Fodder: Report." *NDTV*, November 23, 2015. www.ndtv.com/india-news/indian-recruits-inferior-to-arab-fighters-treated-as-cannon-fodder-report-on-isis-1246695.
2. Gettleman, Jeffrey. "A Mysterious Act of Mercy by the Subway Bombing Suspect." *The New York Times*, December 18, 2017. www.nytimes.com/2017/12/18/world/asia/bangladesh-akayed-ullah-subway-bomber.html.
3. Cohen, Shawn, Abigail Gepner, and Igor Kossov. "Port Authority bombing suspect was 'always angry.'" *New York Post*, December 11, 2017. nypost.com/2017/12/11/neighbors-say-port-authority-bombing-suspect-always-looked-angry/.
4. "Remarks by the President in Address to the Nation on Immigration." The White House, Office of the Press Secretary, press release, November 20, 2014. www.whitehouse.gov/the-press-office/2014/11/20/remarks-president-address-nation-immigration.
5. Esipova, Neli, Julie Ray, and Anita Pugliese. "Number of Potential Migrants Worldwide Tops 700 Million." *Gallup*, June 8, 2017. news.gallup.com/poll/211883/number-potential-migrants-worldwide-tops-700-million.aspx.

6. Esipova, Neli and Julie Ray. "Nearly 700 Million Worldwide Desire to Migrate Permanently." *Gallup.* www.umdcipe.org /conferences/Maastricht/conf_papers/Papers/Gallup-Most _Desired_Migration_Destinations.pdf.

CHAPTER ONE: THE UNFINISHED MELTING POT

1. Hollinger, David S., "Amalgamation and Hypodescent: The Question of Ethnoracial Mixture in the History of the United States," *The American Historical Review* 108:5, December 2003: 1,363–90.
2. Glazer, Nathan. *We Are All Multiculturalists Now.* Cambridge, MA: Harvard University Press, 1998.
3. Lind, Michael. "How to fix America's identity crisis." *Politico,* July 4, 2016. www.politico.com/magazine/story/2016/07/a-new -american-melting-pot-214011.
4. Codevilla, Angelo. "The cold civil war." *Claremont Review of Books,* April 25, 2017. www.claremont.org/crb/article/the-cold -civil-war/.
5. Leyden, Peter and Ruy Teixeira. "The Great Lesson of California in America's New Civil War." *Medium,* January 19, 2018. https:// medium.com/s/state-of-the-future/the-great-lesson-of -california-in-americas-new-civil-war-e52e2861f30.
6. "New Census Bureau Report Analyzes U.S. Population Projections." United States Census Bureau, press release, March 3, 2015. www.census.gov/newsroom/press-releases/2015/cb15 -tps16.html.
7. Wilson, Valerie. "People of color will be a majority of the American working class in 2032." *Economic Policy Institute,* June 9, 2016. www.epi.org/publication/the-changing-demographics-of -americas-working-class/.
8. Gao, George. "Biggest share of whites in U.S. are Boomers, but for minority groups it's Millennials or younger." *Pew Research Center,* July 7, 2016. www.pewresearch.org/fact-tank/2016/07/07 /biggest-share-of-whites-in-u-s-are-boomers-but-for-minority -groups-its-millennials-or-younger/.
9. Romano, Andrew and Garance Franke-Ruta. "A new generation of anti-gentrification radicals are on the march in Los Angeles—and around the country." *Yahoo News,* March 5, 2018. www.yahoo.com /news/new-generation-anti-gentrification-radicals-march-los -angeles-around-country-100000522.html.

10. Vega, Tanzina. "Why the racial wealth gap won't go away." *CNN Money,* January 26, 2016. money.cnn.com/2016/01/25/news /economy/racial-wealth-gap/index.html.

11. Romano, Andrew and Garance Frankie-Ruta. "A New Generation Of Anti-Gentrification Radicals Are On The March In Los Angeles—And Around The Country." *HuffPost.* https:// www.huffingtonpost.com/entry/a-new-generation-of-anti -gentrification-radicals-are-on-the-march-in-los-angeles -and-around-the-country-us_5a9d6c45e4b0479c0255adec.

12. Wealth and Asset Management Services. "The 'Greater' Wealth Transfer." *Accenture.* www.accenture.com/us-en/~/media /Accenture/Conversion-Assets/DotCom/Documents/Global /PDF/Industries_5/Accenture-CM-AWAMS-Wealth-Transfer -Final-June2012-Web-Version.pdf.

13. Emmons, William R., Ana H. Kent, and Lowell R. Ricketts. "The Financial Returns from College across Generations: Large but Unequal." The Federal Reserve Bank of St. Louis. www.stlouisfed .org/~/media/Files/PDFs/HFS/essays/HFS_essay_1-2018.pdf.

14. Stanford University. "Lifting barriers to citizenship for low -income immigrants." Phys.org, January 15, 2018. phys.org/news /2018-01-barriers-citizenship-low-income-immigrants.html.

15. Trevelyan, Edward. "Immigrant Voting in the United States." United States Census Bureau, November 30, 2018. census.gov /newsroom/blogs/random-samplings/2016/11/immigrant _votingin.html.

16. Reeves, Richard V. and Camille Busette. "The middle class is becoming race-plural, just like the rest of America." *Brookings,* February 27, 2018. www.brookings.edu/blog/social-mobility -memos/2018/02/27/the-middle-class-is-becoming-race-plural -just-like-the-rest-of-america/.

17. Williams, Conor. "Williams: Trump's America Through the Fearful but Still Hopeful Eyes of My Old Brooklyn Student & Friends." *The 74 Million,* December 17, 2017. www.the74million .org/article/williams-trumps-america-through-the-fearful-but -still-hopeful-eyes-of-my-old-brooklyn-student-friends/.

CHAPTER TWO: SOMEBODY ELSE'S BABIES

1. Schleifer, Theodore. "King doubles down on controversial 'babies' tweet." *CNN Politics,* March 14, 2017. www.cnn.com/2017/03/13 /politics/steve-king-babies-tweet-cnntv/index.html.

2. "Fertility of foreign-born women remains far higher than that of U.S.-born women." Pew Research Center, October 25, 2016. www .pewsocialtrends.org/2016/10/26/births-outside-of-marriage -decline-for-immigrant-women/st_2016-10-26_fertility_0-04/.

3. Bakalar, Nicholas. "U.S. Fertility Rate Reaches a Record Low." *The New York Times,* July 3, 2017. www.nytimes.com/2017/07/03 /health/united-states-fertility-rate.html.

4. "Fertility of foreign-born women . . ."

5. McCarthy, Niall. "Which Countries Have The Highest Rates of Child Poverty?" *Forbes,* January 16, 2016. www.forbes.com/sites /niallmccarthy/2016/01/04/which-countries-have-the-highest -rates-of-child-poverty-infographic/#40d5ca1f1c68.

6. Hymowitz, Kay S. "Why America Can't Lower Child-Poverty Rates." *City Journal,* Autumn 2017. www.city-journal.org/html /why-america-cant-lower-child-poverty-rates-15498.html.

7. Ibid.

8. Race for Results 2018 Policy Report. The Annie E. Casey Foundation. www.aecf.org/m/resourcedoc/aecf -2017raceforresults-2017.pdf.

9. Ibid.

10. Ibid.

11. Ibid.

12. Waters, Mary C. and Marisa Gerstein Pineau, eds. *The Integration of Immigrants into American Society.* Washington, DC: The National Academic Press, 2015.

13. Duncan, Brian and Stephen J. Trejo. "Assessing the Socioeconomic Mobility and Integration of U.S. Immigrants and Their Descendants." *The ANNALS of the American Academy of Political and Social Science* 657:1 (December 10, 2014): 108–135. doi .org/10.1177/0002716214548396.

14. Lichter, Daniel T., Scott R. Sanders, and Kenneth M. Johnson. "Hispanics at the Starting Line: Poverty among Newborn Infants in Established Gateways and New Destinations." *Social Forces* 94:1 (September 1, 2015): 209–235. doi.org/10.1093/sf/sov043.

15. Feliciano, Cynthia. *Unequal Origins: Immigrant Selection and the Education of the Second Generation.* El Paso, TX: LFB Scholarly Publishing, 2008.

16. Chakravorty, Sanjoy, Devesh Kapur, and Nirvikar Singh. *The Other One Percent: Indians in America.* Oxford, UK: Oxford University Press, 2017.

17. Lazear, Edward. "Why Are Some Immigrant Groups More
    Successful than Others?" NBER Working Paper No. 23548,
    October 2017. http://www.nber.org/papers/w23548.
18. Joo, Nathan and Richard V. Reeves. "How upwardly mobile are
    Hispanic children? Depends on how you look at it." *Brookings*,
    November 10, 2015. www.brookings.edu/blog/social-mobility
    -memos/2015/11/10/how-upwardly-mobile-are-hispanic
    -children-depends-how-you-look-at-it/.
19. Duncan and Trejo.
20. Waters and Pineau.
21. Ibid.
22. Lubotsky, Darren. "Chutes or Ladders? A Longitudinal Analysis
    of Immigrant Earnings." *Journal of Political Economy* 115:5 (October
    2007): 820–67. doi.org/10.1086/522871.
23. Waters and Pineau.
24. Ibid.
25. Ibid.
26. National Academies of Sciences, Engineering, and Medicine. *The
    Economic and Fiscal Consequences of Immigration.* Washington, DC:
    The National Academies Press, 2017. doi.org/10.17226/23550.
27. Duncan, Brian and Stephen J. Trejo. "Assessing the
    Socioeconomic Mobility and Integration of U.S. Immigrants and
    Their Descendants." *The ANNALS of the American Academy of
    Political and Social Science* 657 (January 2015). http://journals
    .sagepub.com/doi/abs/10.1177/0002716214548396.
28. Bitler, Marianne P., Annie Laurie Hines, and Marianne Page.
    "Cash for Kids." *The Russell Sage Foundation Journal of the Social
    Sciences* 4:2 (2018): 43–73. www.rsfjournal.org/doi/full/10.7758
    /RSF.2018.4.2.03.
29. Rothstein, Jesse. "Equal access to a good education is not just
    about sound school budgets." Washington Center for Equitable
    Growth, April 23, 2018. http://equitablegrowth.org/research
    -analysis/equal-access-to-a-good-education-is-not-just-about
    -sound-school-budgets/.
30. Jones, Robert P., Daniel Cox, and Juhem Navarro-Rivera. "How
    Shifting Religious Identities and Experiences Are Influencing
    Hispanic Approaches to Politics." Public Religion Research Institute,
    2013. www.prri.org/research/hispanic-values-survey-2013/.
31. Williams, Erica and Samantha Waxman. "State Earned Income
    Tax Credits and Minimum Wages Work Best Together." Center on

Budget and Policy Priorities, February 7, 2018. www.cbpp.org
/research/state-budget-and-tax/state-earned-income-tax-credits
-and-minimum-wages-work-best-together.

32. "Public Charge Fact Sheet." U.S. Citizenship and Immigration
Services, Niskanen Center, April 29, 2011. www.uscis.gov/news
/fact-sheets/public-charge-fact-sheet.

33. Salam, Reihan. "Keep Your Tired, Your Poor, Your Huddled
Masses." *Slate*, February 2, 2017. www.slate.com/articles/news
_and_politics/politics/2017/02/how_radical_is_donald_trump_s
_immigration_agenda.html.

34. Hammond, Samuel and Robert Orr. "Redefining 'Public Charge':
Gauging the Threat to Noncitizens from Trump's Draft EO."
Niskanen Center. niskanencenter.org/wp-content/uploads/2017
/02/Redefining_Public_Charge.pdf.

35. Hammond, Samuel and Robert Orr. "The Myth of the
Government-Dependent Immigrant Poor Noncitizens Use Public
Benefits at Much Lower Rates Than Poor Citizens." Niskanen
Center. niskanencenter.org/wp-content/uploads/2017/02
/NoncitizenPublicBenefits.pdf.

36. East, Chloe N. "The Effect of Food Stamps on Children's Health:
Evidence from Immigrants' Changing Eligibility." dissertation,
University of Colorado Denver, August 6, 2017. www.chloeeast
.com/uploads/8/9/9/7/8997263/east_fskids_r_r.pdf.

37. Sherman, Arloc and Danilo Trisi. "Safety Net for Poorest
Weakened After Welfare Law But Regained Strength in Great
Recession, at Least Temporarily." Center on Budget and Policy
Priorities, March 11, 2015. www.cbpp.org/research/poverty-and
-inequality/safety-net-for-poorest-weakened-after-welfare-law
-but-regained.

38. National Academies of Sciences, Engineering, and Medicine. *The
Economic and Fiscal Consequences of Immigration*, 2017. Washington,
DC: The National Academies Press. doi.org/10.17226/23550.

39. Hoynes, Hilary W., Diane Whitmore Schanzenbach, and
Douglas Almond. "Long Run Impacts of Childhood Access to
the Safety Net." University of California Berkeley. gspp.berkeley
.edu/assets/uploads/research/pdf/Hoynes-Schanzenbach
-Almond-4-14.pdf.

40. National Academies of Sciences, Engineering, and Medicine.

41. Ibid.

42. Ibid.

43. Salam, Reihan. "The Case for Skills-Based Immigration." *National Review*, August 28, 2017. www.nationalreview.com/2017/08/ skills-based-immigration-works-todays-economy/.

44. National Academies of Sciences, Engineering, and Medicine.

45. Capps, Randy, Michael Fix, and Jie Zong. "A Profile of U.S. Children with Unauthorized Immigrant Parents." *Migration Policy Institute*, January 2016. www.migrationpolicy.org/research /profile-us-children-unauthorized-immigrant-parents.

46. Toppa, Sabrina. "How migrant mothers in Qatar work for a pittance, far away from their children." *Middle East Eye*, January 11, 2018. www.middleeasteye.net/news/qatar-s-female-migrant -workers-struggle-between-motherhood-and-work-2107371605.

47. "Qatar to approve permanent residency for some experts." *Al Jazeera*, August 3, 2017. www.aljazeera.com/news/2017/08/qatar -approve-permanent-residency-expats-170803095052801.html.

48. Ruhs, Martin. *The Price of Rights*. Princeton, NJ: Princeton University Press, 2013.

49. Matthews, Dylan. "The case for open borders." *Vox*, December 15, 2014. www.vox.com/2014/9/13/6135905/open-borders-bryan -caplan-interview-gdp-double.

50. Conn, David. "Thousands of Qatar World Cup workers 'subjected to life-threatening heat.'" *The Guardian*, September 26, 2017. www .theguardian.com/football/2017/sep/27/thousands-qatar-world -cup-workers-life-threatening-heat.

51. Gest, Justin. "How America Fell Behind the World on Immigration." *Politico*, March 19, 2018. www.politico.com /magazine/story/2018/03/19/how-america-fell-behind-the -world-on-immigration-217658.

52. Bui, Quoctrung and Caitlin Dickerson. "What Can the U.S. Learn From How Other Countries Handle Immigration?" *The New York Times*, February 16, 2018. www.nytimes.com/interactive/2018/02 /16/upshot/comparing-immigration-policies-across-countries.html.

CHAPTER THREE: RACE TO THE BOTTOM

1. Krogstad, Jens Manuel and Ana Gonzalez-Barrera. "A majority of English-speaking Hispanics in the U.S. are bilingual." *Pew Research Center*, March 24, 2018. www.pewresearch.org/fact-tank/2015/03 /24/a-majority-of-english-speaking-hispanics-in-the-u-s-are -bilingual.

2. Inspired by Richard Alba.

3. Alba, Richard. "The Likely Persistence of a White Majority." *American Prospect*, January 11, 2016. prospect.org/article/likely-persistence-white-majority-0.

4. Lind, Michael. *The Next American Nation: The New Nationalism & the Fourth American Revolution.* New York: Free Press, 1996.

5. Alba, Richard, Tomás R. Jiménez, and Helen B. Marrow. "Mexican Americans as a paradigm for contemporary intra-group heterogeneity." *Ethnic and Racial Studies* 37:3 (2014): 446–66.

6. Bald, Vivek. *Bengali Harlem and the Lost Histories of South Asian America.* Cambridge, MA: Harvard University Press, 2015.

7. Alba, Richard. *Blurring the Color Line: The New Chance for a More Integrated America.* Cambridge, MA: Harvard University Press, 2015.

8. Cowie, Jefferson. *The Great Exception: The New Deal & the Limits of American Politics.* Princeton, NJ: Princeton University Press, 2016.

9. Massey.

10. Kammer, Jerry. *What Happened to Worksite Enforcement?* Center for Immigration Studies, 2017.

11. Hanson, George, Chen Liu, and Craig McIntosh. "Along the watchtower: The rise and fall of U.S. low-skilled immigration." *Brookings Papers on Economic Activity*, BPEA Conference Drafts, March 23–24, 2017. www.brookings.edu/wp-content/uploads/2017/03/2_hansonetal.pdf.

12. "Larger share of unauthorized immigrants are long-term residents." Pew Research Center, September 19, 2016. www.pewhispanic.org/2016/09/20/overall-number-of-u-s-unauthorized-immigrants-holds-steady-since-2009/ph_2016-09-20_unauthorized-04/.

13 Salam, Reihan. "Republicans Need a New Approach to Immigration." *National Review*, January 4, 2016. www.nationalreview.com/2016/01/immigration-new-culture-war/.

14. Jimenez RE.

15. Qiao, Zhenchao and Daniel T. Lichter. "Social Boundaries and Marital Assimilation: Interpreting Trends in Racial and Ethnic Intermarriage." *American Sociological Review* 72: 1, 2007. http://journals.sagepub.com/doi/10.1177/000312240707200104.

16. Lopez, Mark Hugo, Ana Gonzalez-Barrera, and Gustavo López. "Hispanic Identity Fades Across Generations as Immigrant Connections Fall Away." Pew Research Center, December 20, 2017. www.pewhispanic.org/2017/12/20/hispanic-identity-fades-across-generations-as-immigrant-connections-fall-away/.

17. Abrajano, Marisa and Zoltan L. Hajnal. *White Backlash: Immigration, Race, and American Politics.* Oxford, UK: Oxford University Press, 2015.

18. Adida, Claire L., David D. Laitin, and Marie-Anne Valfort. "Don't fear Muslim immigrants." *Foreign Affairs,* Apil 26, 2016. www .foreignaffairs.com/articles/united-states/2016-04-26/dont-fear -muslim-immigrants.

CHAPTER FOUR: JOBS ROBOTS WILL DO

1. Baldwin, Richard. *The Great Convergence.* Cambridge, MA: Harvard University Press, 2016.

2. "Refugees in Sweden: Seeking asylum—and jobs." *The Economist,* November 6, 2016. www.economist.com/news/finance-economics /21709511-too-few-refugees-not-too-many-are-working-europe -refugees-sweden-are, and "Immigration is Changing the Swedish Welfare State." *The Economist,* June 8, 2017. www.economist.com /europe/2017/06/08/immigration-is-changing-the-swedish -welfare-state.

3. Ibid.

4. Ibid.

5. Roman, David and Chanyaporn Chanjaroen. "Why Singapore Wants Its Food Courts to Be Run by Machines, Not People." *Bloomberg,* October 30, 2016. www.bloomberg.com/news/articles /2016-10-30/singapore-food-courts-are-ground-zero-in -productivity-revolution.

6. Gest, Justin. "How America Fell Behind the World on Immigration." *Politico,* March 19, 2018. www.politico.com /magazine/story/2018/03/19/how-america-fell-behind-the -world-on-immigration-217658.

7. Bhattacharya, Ananya. "Singapore First: Quietly shutting the door on Indian techies and other foreign workers." *Quartz India,* April 12, 2017. qz.com/950172/the-us-isnt-the-only-country-shutting -the-door-on-indian-techies/.

8. Lewis, Ethan. "How Immigration Affects Workers: Two Wrong Models and a Right One." *Cato Journal* 37:3 (Fall 2017). object.cato .org/sites/cato.org/files/serials/files/cato-journal/2017/9/cato -journal-v37n3-3.pdf.

9. Ibid.

10. "Why Samsung of South Korea is the biggest firm in Vietnam." *The Economist,* April 12, 2018. www.economist.com/news/asia

/21740430-it-makes-most-its-smartphones-there-why-samsung
-south-korea-biggest-firm-vietnam.

11. Salam, Reihan. "Trump Can't Have It Both Ways." *The Atlantic*,
    March 2, 2018. www.theatlantic.com/politics/archive/2018/03
    /trumps-economic-nationalism/554732/.

12. Peters, Margaret E. *Trading Barriers: Immigration and the Remaking of
    Globalization.* Princeton, NJ: Princeton University Press, 2017.

13. Cortés, Patricia and José Tessada. "Low-Skilled Immigration and
    the Labor Supply of Highly Skilled Women." *American Economic
    Journal: Applied Economics* 3:3 (July 2011): 88–123. www.aeaweb.org
    /articles?id=10.1257/app.3.3.88.

14. Pritchett, Lant. "Why Are Geniuses Destroying Jobs in Uganda?"
    Center for Global Development, June 15, 2017. www.cgdev.org/blog
    /why-are-geniuses-destroying-jobs-uganda.

15. Ibid.

16. Ibid.

17. Allen, Robert. "Why Was the Industrial Revolution British?" *Vox
    EU*, May 15, 2009. voxeu.org/article/why-was-industrial
    -revolution-british.

18. Lewis, Ethan. "Immigration, Skill Mix, and Capital Skill Com-
    plementarity." *The Quarterly Journal of Economics* 2 (1 May 2011):
    1,029–69. https://doi.org/10.1093/qje/qjr011.

19. Basso, Gaetano, Giovanni Peri, and Ahmed Rahman. "The impact
    of immigration on wage distributions in the era of technical
    automation." *Vox EU,* January 12, 2018. voxeu.org/article
    /immigration-era-automation.

20. Posner, Eric and Glen Weyl. "Sponsor An Immigrant Yourself."
    Politico, February 13, 2018. www.politico.com/magazine/story
    /2018/02/13/immigration-visas-economics-216968.

21. Posner, Eric A. and Glen Weyl. "A Radical Solution to Global
    Income Inequality: Make the U.S. More Like Qatar." *New Republic*,
    November 6, 2014. newrepublic.com/article/120179/how-reduce
    -global-income-inequality-open-immigration-policies.

22. Pethokoukis, James. "Why the US might need those Mexican
    high-school dropouts." American Enterprise Institute, June 26,
    2013. www.aei.org/publication/why-the-us-might-need-those
    -mexican-high-school-dropouts/.

23. Bivens, Josh. "A 'high-pressure economy' can help boost productivity
    and provide even more 'room to run' for the recovery." *Economic
    Policy Institute*, March 12, 2017. www.epi.org/publication/a-high

-pressure-economy-can-help-boost-productivity-and-provide
-even-more-room-to-run-for-the-recovery/.

24. Levitz, Jennifer. "To Fill Summer Jobs, Maine Gov. Releases
Nonviolent Prisoners." *The Wall Street Journal*, May 31, 2017. www
.wsj.com/articles/to-fill-summer-jobs-maine-gov-releases
-nonviolent-prisoners-1496256090.

25. Mohan, Geoffrey. "As California's labor shortage grows, farmers
race to replace workers with robots." *Los Angeles Times*, July 21,
2017. www.latimes.com/projects/la-fi-farm-mechanization/.

26. Horton, John J. "AI, Labor, and the Parable of the Horse." May 10,
2017. john-joseph-horton.com/ai-labor-and-the-parable-of-the
-horse/.

27. West, Darrell M. "Will robots and AI take your job? The
economic and political consequences of automation." Brookings
Institution, April 18, 2018. https://www.brookings.edu/blog
/techtank/2018/04/18/will-robots-and-ai-take-your-job
-the-economic-and-political-consequences-of-automation/.

28. Olsen, Henry. "A New Homestead Act—To Jump Start the U.S.
Economy." *National Interest*, December 15, 2015. eppc.org/publi
cations/a-new-homestead-act-to-jump-start-the-u-s-economy/.

29. Cadena, Brian C., and Brian K. Kovak. "Immigrants Equilibrate
Local Labor Markets: Evidence from the Great Recession."
American Economic Journal: Applied Economics 8:1 (2016): 257–90.

CHAPTER FIVE: IT'S A SMALL WORLD

1. Clemens, Michael. "Does Development Reduce Migration?"
Center for Global Development, 2014. www.cgdev.org/sites
/default/files/does-development-reduce-migration_final
_0.pdf.

2. Ibid.

3. Kochhar, Rakesh. "10 projections for the global population in
2050." Pew Research Center, February 3, 2014. www.pewresearch
.org/fact-tank/2014/02/03/10-projections-for-the-global
-population-in-2050/.

4. Quintana, Ana. "U.S. Foreign Assistance to Mexico, Guatemala,
Honduras, and El Salvador." Heritage Foundation, July 8, 2014.
www.heritage.org/global-politics/report/us-foreign-assistance
-mexico-guatemala-honduras-and-el-salvador.

5. Salam, Reihan. "Beyond the Wall." *National Review*, March 28, 2016. www.nationalreview.com/magazine/2016/03/28/beyond-wall/.

6. Grant, Charley. "Alzheimer's: Pharma's Great White Whale Is Still Worth Hunting." *The Wall Street Journal*, February 20, 2017. www.wsj.com/articles/alzheimers-pharmas-great-white-whale-is-still-worth-hunting-1487599380.

7. Agronin, Marc. "How to Reduce Dementia's Tragic Toll on Families." *The Wall Street Journal*, November 12, 2017. www.wsj.com/articles/how-to-reduce-dementias-tragic-toll-on-families-1510542660.

8. Verdery, Ashton M. and Rachel Margolis. "Projections of white and black older adults without living kin in the United States, 2015 to 2060." *Proceedings of the National Academy of Sciences* 114:42 (October 2017): 11,109–114. https://doi.org/10.1073/pnas.1710341114.

9. Castañeda, Jorge G. *Ex Mex: Mexicans in the US, from Migrants to Immigrants*. New York: The New Press, 2008.

10. Lind, Dara. "Migrant caravans, Trump's latest immigration obsession, explained." *Vox*, April 6, 2018. www.vox.com/policy-and-politics/2018/4/6/17206042/caravan-mexico-trump-rape.

11. Hanson, Gordon and Craig McIntosh. "Is the Mediterranean the New Rio Grande? US and EU Immigration Pressures in the Long Run." *Journal of Economic Perspectives* 30:4 (Fall 2016): 1–25. gps.ucsd.edu/_files/faculty/hanson/hanson_publication_immigration_mediterranean.pdf.

12. Ibid.

13. "Poverty and Shared Prosperity 2016: Taking on Inequality." The World Bank, 2016. openknowledge.worldbank.org/bitstream/handle/10986/25078/9781464809583.pdf.

14. "World population projected to reach 9.8 billion in 2050, and 11.2 billion in 2100—says UN." Sustainable Development Goals, United Nations. www.un.org/sustainabledevelopment/blog/2017/06/world-population-projected-to-reach-9-8-billion-in-2050-and-11-2-billion-in-2100-says-un/.

15. Chandramouli, C. "Rural Urban Distribution of Population." Census of India 2011, July 15, 2011. censusindia.gov.in/2011-prov-results/paper2/data_files/india/Rural_Urban_2011.pdf.

16. Padmanabhan, Anil. "Urban inequality rising far more in India: François Bourguignon." Livemint. May 23, 2015. www.livemint.com/Politics/5JVPBWc7VGX0AMt3U3YeQM/Urban-inequality-increasing-far-more-in-India-Franois-Bour.html.

17. "Urbanization in India." World Bank report, September 22, 2011. www.worldbank.org/en/news/feature/2011/09/22/india -urbanization.

18. Malik, Ajaz Ahmad. "Urbanization and Crime: A Relational Analysis." *IOSR Journal of Humanities and Social Science* 21:1, Ver. IV (January 2016): 68–74. www.iosrjournals.org/iosr-jhss/papers /Vol.%2021%20Issue1/Version-4/G021146874.pdf.

19. United Nations. *World Urbanization Prospects: The 2014 Revision, Highlights.* Department of Economic and Social Affairs, Population Division (2014). esa.un.org/unpd/wup/publications/files /wup2014-highlights.pdf.

20. Hanson, George, Chen Liu, and Craig McIntosh. "Along the watchtower: The rise and fall of U.S. low-skilled immigration." *Brookings Papers on Economic Activity*, from the BPEA Conference Drafts, March 23–24, 2017. www.brookings.edu/wp-content /uploads/2017/03/2_hansonetal.pdf.

21. Kharas, Homi. "The Unprecedented Expansion of the Global Middle Class." Global Economy and Development. Working Paper 100, February 2017. www.brookings.edu/wp -content/uploads/2017/02/global_20170228_global-middle-class .pdf.

22. Fuller, Brandon and Paul Romer. "Urbanization as Opportunity" in *Rethinking Cities: A Roadmap Toward Better Urbanization for Development.* Edward Glaeser and Abha Joshi-Ghani, eds., World Bank, 2014. paulromer.net/wp-content/uploads/2014/02 /Urbanization-As-Opportunity-Marron-Version.pdf.

23. Mallaby, Sebastian. "The Politically Incorrect Guide to Ending Poverty." *The Atlantic,* July/August 2010. www.theatlantic.com /magazine/archive/2010/07/the-politically-incorrect-guide-to -ending-poverty/308134/.

24. Abadi, Cameron. "The Dam Will Hold. Until It Doesn't." *Foreign Policy,* October 6, 2017. europeslamsitsgates.foreignpolicy.com /part-5-the-dam-will-hold-until-it-doesnt-germany-europe -merkel-EU-africa-migration.

25. Kingsley, Patrick. "Migration between poor countries rising faster than to rich ones—study." *The Guardian,* April 20, 2016. www .theguardian.com/world/2016/apr/20/migration-between-poor -countries-rising-faster-than-to-rich-ones-study.

26. "The other kind of immigration." *The Economist,* December 24, 2016. www.economist.com/news/international/21712137-flow -people-poor-countries-other-poor-countries-little-noticed.

27. Betts, Alexander and Paul Collier. "Help Refugees Help Themselves." *Foreign Affairs*, November/December 2015. www .foreignaffairs.com/articles/levant/2015-10-20/help-refugees -help-themselves.

28. Salam, Reihan. "Resettling Syrian Refugees: An Alternative." *Slate*, November 16, 2015. www.slate.com/articles/news_and _politics/politics/2015/11/syrian_refugee_crisis_an_alternative _to_resettling_refugees_in_europe.html/.

29. Collier, Paul and Alexander Betts. "Why denying refugees the right to work is a catastrophic error." *The Guardian*. March 22, 2017. www.theguardian.com/world/2017/mar/22/why-denying -refugees-the-right-to-work-is-a-catastrophic-error.

30. Baldwin, Richard. *The Great Convergence: Information Technology and the New Globalization*. Cambridge, MA: Belknap Press, 2016.

31. Clemens, Michael, Claudio E. Montenegro, and Lant Pritchett. "The Place Premium: Wage Differences for Identical Workers across the U.S. Border." Working Papers, Center for Global Development, July 3, 2008. www.cgdev.org/publication/place -premium-wage-differences-identical-workers-across-us-border -working-paper-148.

32. Singer, Peter. "Is Extreme Poverty Being Neglected in the U.S.?" *The New York Times*, January 28, 2018. www.nytimes.com/2018 /01/28/opinion/extreme-poverty-us.html.

33. New World Encyclopedia. "J. B. S. Haldane." www .newworldencyclopedia.org/entry/J._B._S._Haldane.

34. Easterbrook, Gregg. "Forgotten Benefactor of Humanity." *The Atlantic*, January 1997. www.theatlantic.com/magazine/archive /1997/01/forgotten-benefactor-of-humanity/306101/.

CHAPTER SIX: NATION BUILDING

1. Tyson, Alec. "Public backs legal status for immigrants brought to U.S. illegally as children, but not a bigger border wall." Pew Research Center, January 19, 2018. www.pewresearch.org/fact-tank /2018/01/19/public-backs-legal-status-for-immigrants-brought -to-u-s-illegally-as-children-but-not-a-bigger-border-wall/.

2. Wright, Matthew, Morris Levy, and Jack Citrin. "Public Attitudes Toward Immigration Policy Across the Legal/Illegal Divide: The Role of Categorical and Attribute-Based Decision-Making." *Political Behavior* 38:1 (March 1, 2016). cloudfront.escholarship.org /dist/prd/content/qt19m3r9c7/qt19m3r9c7.pdf.

3. Wright, Matthew. "Ahead of government shutdown, Congress sets its sights on not-so-comprehensive immigration reform." *The Conversation,* January 18, 2018. theconversation.com/ahead-of -government-shutdown-congress-sets-its-sights-on-not-so -comprehensive-immigration-reform-89998.

4. Krogstad, Jens Manuel, Jeffrey S. Passel, and D'Vera Cohn. "5 facts about illegal immigration in the U.S." Pew Research Center, April 27, 2017. www.pewresearch.org/fact-tank/2017/04/27 /5-facts-about-illegal-immigration-in-the-u-s/.

5. Cox and Posner.

6. Skerry, Peter. "Splitting the Differences on Illegal Immigration." *National Affairs* 35 (Spring 2018). www.nationalaffairs.com /publications/detail/splitting-the-difference-on-illegal -immigration.

7. Martin, David A. "Resolute Enforcement Is Not Just for Restrictionists: Building a Stable and Efficient Immigration Enforcement System." *Journal of Law and Politics* 30:411 (2014–2015): 411–64. content.law.virginia.edu/system/files/faculty/hein/2015 /Martin30JLPol411.pdf.

8. "Breaking the Immigration Stalemate: From Deep Disagreements to Constructive Proposals." Brookings-Duke Immigration Policy Roundtable, October 6, 2009. kenan.ethics.duke.edu/wp-content /uploads/2012/08/Brookings-Duke-Breaking-the-Immigration -Stalemate.pdf.

9. Citrin, Jack, Morris Levy, and Matthew Wright. "Trump wants an immigration system overhaul. Do Americans agree?" *The Washington Post,* April 3, 2017. www.washingtonpost.com/news /monkey-cage/wp/2017/04/03/trump-wants-an-immigration -system-overhaul-do-americans-agree/?utm_term=.105d63 c53e0a.

10. Batalova, Jeanne and Michael Fix. "New Brain Gain: Rising Human Capital among Recent Immigrants to the United States." Migration Policy Institute, June 2017. www.migrationpolicy.org /research/new-brain-gain-rising-human-capital-among-recent -immigrants-united-states.

11. Ibid.

12. Ibid.

13. Ibid.

14. Hanushek, Eric A. and Ludger Wöesmann. "Education Quality and Economic Growth." The World Bank, 2017. siteresources .worldbank.org/EDUCATION/Resources/278200

-1099079877269/547664-1099079934475/Edu_Quality_Economic
_Growth.pdf.

15. Camarota, Steven A. "Welfare Use by Immigrant and Native
    Households: An Analysis of Medicaid, Cash, Food, and Housing
    Programs." Center for Immigration Studies, September 10, 2015.
    cis.org/Report/Welfare-Use-Immigrant-and-Native-Households.

16. Kandel, William A. "U.S. Family-Based Immigration Policy."
    Congressional Research Service, February 19, 2018. fas.org/sgp
    /crs/homesec/R43145.pdf.

17. Tienda, Marta. "Health and Age of Immigrants Admitted to the
    U.S. Matter." *The New York Times*, May 13, 2017. www.nytimes.com
    /roomfordebate/2013/04/16/the-economics-of-immigration
    /health-and-age-of-immigrants-admitted-to-the-us-matter.

18. Cox, Adam B. and Eric A. Posner. "The Second Order Structure
    of Immigration Law." *Stanford Law Review* 59:4 (2007); University
    of Chicago, Public Law Working Paper No. 140; University
    Chicago Law & Economics, Olin Working Paper No. 314. ssrn
    .com/abstract=941730.

19. Hammond, Samuel. "Redefining 'Public Charge' and the Threat
    to Noncitizens." Niskanen Center, February 10, 2017.
    niskanencenter.org/blog/redefining-public-charge-threat
    -noncitizens/.

20. Cohn, D'Vera and Neil G. Ruiz. " More than half of new green
    cards go to people already living in the U.S." Pew Research
    Center, July 6, 2017. www.pewresearch.org/fact-tank/2017/07/06
    /more-than-half-of-new-green-cards-go-to-people-already
    -living-in-the-u-s/.

21. Hainmueller, Jens and Daniel J. Hopkins. "The Hidden American
    Immigration Consensus: A Conjoint Analysis of Attitudes Toward
    Immigrants." *American Journal of Political Science* 59:3 (2015):
    529–48.

22. Capps, Randy, Michael Fix, Jennifer Van Hook, and James D.
    Bachmeier. "A Demographic, Socioeconomic, and Health Coverage
    Profile of Unauthorized Immigrants in the United States."
    Migration Policy Institute, May 2013. www.migrationpolicy.org
    /research/demographic-socioeconomic-and-health-coverage
    -profile-unauthorized-immigrants-united-states.

23. Ibid.

24. Hanson, George, Chen Liu, and Craig McIntosh. "Along the
    watchtower: The rise and fall of U.S. low-skilled immigration."
    Brookings Papers on Economic Activity, BPEA Conference Drafts,

March 23–24, 2017. www.brookings.edu/wp-content/uploads /2017/03/2_hansonetal.pdf.

25. Shaefer, Luke H., Sophie Collyer, Greg Duncan, Kathryn Edin, Irwin Garfinkel, David Harris, Timothy M. Smeeding, Jane Waldfogel, Christopher Wimer, Hirokazu Yoshikawa. "A Universal Child Allowance: A Plan to Reduce Poverty and Income Instability Among Children in the United States." *RSF: The Russell Sage Foundation Journal of the Social Sciences* 4:2 (February 2018): 22–42.

26. Ibid.

27. Bitler, Marianne P., Annie Laurie Hines, and Marianne Page. "Cash for Kids." *RSF: The Russell Sage Foundation Journal of the Social Sciences* 42 (2018): 43–73.

28. Shaefer et al.

29. Bitler et al.

30. Hoynes, Hilary W., Douglas L. Miller, and David Simon. "Income, the Earned Income Tax Credit, and Infant Health." *American Economic Journal: Economic Policy* 7:1 (2012): 172–211.

31. Dahl, Gordon B. and Lance Lochner. "The Impact of Family Income on Child Achievement: Evidence from the Earned Income Tax Credit." *American Economic Review* 102:5 (August 2012): 1,927–56.

32. Shaefer et al.

33. Bitler et al.

34. Shaefer et al.

INDEX

WITHDRAWN

DATE DUE

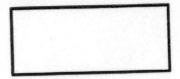

**This item is Due on
or before Date shown.**

DEC - - 2018